Opening to Our Primordial Nature

Opening to Our Primordial Nature

by

Khenchen Palden Sherab Rinpoche

and

Khenpo Tsewang Dongyal Rinpoche

Edited by Ann Helm and Michael White

Snow Lion Publications

Ithaca, New York • Boulder, Colorado

Snow Lion Publications
P.O. Box 6483
Ithaca, NY 14851 USA
(607) 273-8519
www.snowlionpub.com

ISBN-10: 1-55939-249-5
ISBN-13: 978-1-55939-249-5

Printed in the United States of America

Library of Congress Cataloging-in-Publication Data

Sherab, Khenchen Palden, Rinpoche, 1941-
   [Light of the three jewels.]
   Opening to our primordial nature / by Khenchen Palden Sherab Rinpoche and Khenpo
Tsewang Dongyal Rinpoche ; edited by Ann Helm and Michael White.-- 2nd ed.
      p. cm.
   "First edition published as Light of the Three Jewels (c) 1998 by Dharma Samudra"--
T.P. verso.
   ISBN-13: 978-1-55939-249-5 (alk. paper)
   ISBN-10: 1-55939-249-5 (alk. paper)
   1. Spiritual life--Buddhism. 2. Spiritual life--Rñiṅ-ma-pa (Sect) 3. Buddhism--
China--Tibet--Doctrines. I. Dongyal, Khenpo Tsewang, Rinpoche, 1951- II. Helm, Ann,
1949- III. White, Michael, 1948- IV. Title.

BQ7775.S54 2006
294.3'4--dc22
                                                                    2006005934

TABLE OF CONTENTS

ACKNOWLEDGMENTS

This book is based on several talks given in Tennessee in 1988 and 1989, as well as additional talks in other areas of the United States. Khenchen Palden Sherab Rinpoche and Khenpo Tsewang Dongyal Rinpoche would like to thank Michael White, Susan White, Ann Helm, and many other sangha members whose work contributed to this book. Thanks also to Nancy Roberts and Rita Frizzell for their assistance in preparing this text for publishing.

May everyone who reads this book understand the value and meaning of their precious life. May their highest aspirations be fulfilled for the benefit of all beings.

Editor's Introduction

It is ironic that the Tibetan Buddhist teachings of love and compassion have come to the West due to the devastation of Tibet by the Chinese Communists. Before the Communist takeover in 1959, Tibet was almost untouched by the industrial age. The Tibetan people lived without electricity, motorized vehicles, modern roads, or advanced weaponry.

The Communist Chinese proclaimed that they were liberating the people of Tibet, yet in the process they practically destroyed the Tibetan monastic culture. Buddhist monks and nuns were presented with painful choices: they could deny their religious convictions, flee the country, or face imprisonment or death. Before the Chinese takeover, Tibet was a country of seven million inhabitants. The invasion resulted in the loss of one million Tibetan lives, the destruction of six thousand monasteries, and the exodus of more than one hundred thousand refugees.

Khenchen Palden Sherab Rinpoche and his brother, Khenpo Tsewang Dongyal Rinpoche, were among the refugees who fled to India and Nepal. Along with their parents and two sisters, they left eastern Tibet in the middle of winter and traveled for eighteen months to reach India. Their journey was fraught with danger — three times they were captured and each time they managed to escape. The journey was too arduous for the women in their family — as they neared the Indian border, one of their sisters died, and their mother and the other sister died soon after they reached the refugee camps in India.

This daring escape cast the two brothers into the modern world. Khenchen Palden Sherab Rinpoche is among the last generation of Tibetans fully educated in the monastic system of old Tibet. When he

Photos, opposite page: (1) The Venerable Khenpos with their father, Lama Chimed; (2) Pema Samye Chökhor Ling Monastery, Sarnath, India; (3) Orgyen Samye Chökhor Ling Nunnery, Sarnath, India; (4) Padma Samye Ling Monastery and Retreat Center, upstate New York; (5) The Great Miracle Stupa, Shravasti, India

speaks of his life in Tibet, he refers to it as "ancient times." These brothers now make their home in New York. It is remarkable that these men, raised in a system of ancient esoteric principles, now find themselves, by a twist of fate, in contemporary America.

Khenchen Palden Sherab Rinpoche was born in 1941 in the village of Gyuphu, in the Doshul region of eastern Tibet near the sacred mountain of Jowo Zegyal. Jowo Zegyal is one of the five mountains in Tibet specifically associated with the five dhyani buddhas and with Guru Padmasambhava, the founder of Tibetan Buddhism. One of Khenchen Rinpoche's ancestors was a direct student of Guru Padmasambhava; other relatives were renowned scholars, practitioners, and tertons. His family inherited the responsibility of administering Gochen Monastery, the local monastery in their region, which was founded by the great terton Tsasum Lingpa.

Khenchen Rinpoche began his education at the age of four when his father, Lama Chimed Namgyal, taught him to read. The first book he read was the life story of Mandarava, a wisdom dakini and consort of Padmasambhava. At the age of six he was chosen to become the next abbot of Gochen Monastery. At the age of seven he completed his first meditation retreat, living with an older monk, Changchub Gyatso, for a month in a stone hut at the base of a glacier on Jowo Zegyal Mountain.

His family was semi-nomadic; they lived in a village house with six other families during the winters, and moved with their yak-hair tents in the summers. At the age of twelve, Khenchen Rinpoche moved to Riwoche Monastery, one of the largest and oldest educational institutions in eastern Tibet. He completed his studies there just as the Chinese invasion reached that area.

In 1965, when he had been a refugee in India for a few years, Khenchen Rinpoche was asked to join a group of scholars and the leaders of the four main schools of Tibetan Buddhism to discuss ways to maintain the culture and religion of Tibet. This conference met periodically over a year's time, and led to the formation of the Central Institute of Higher Tibetan Studies in Sarnath, India. In 1967, Khenchen Rinpoche was appointed head of the Nyingmapa Department of this institute by His Holiness Dudjom Rinpoche, who was the supreme head of the Nyingma lineage from 1960 until his parinirvana in 1987. In 1980, Khenchen Rinpoche and his brother, Khenpo Tsewang Dongyal Rinpoche, made their first trip to the U.S. and began working with H. H. Dudjom Rinpoche in the West.

Khenchen Palden Sherab Rinpoche is the author of works on Tibetan grammar, poetry, philosophy, and history. Several of his books are used in courses at the Central Institute of Higher Tibetan Studies. He has taught in Tibet, India, Nepal, England, France, Belgium, Australia, Canada, Russia, Puerto Rico, and throughout the United States. Khenchen Rinpoche is considered one of the greatest living scholars and meditation masters of Tibetan Nyingma Buddhism.

Khenpo Tsewang Dongyal Rinpoche was born in 1950 in Tibet, in the same area as his brother. Soon after his birth he was recognized as a tulku, the reincarnation of Sherab Khyentse, a renowned abbot of Gochen Monastery. His studies were interrupted by the Chinese invasion and he fled with his family to India. In the early 1960s, Khenpo Tsewang Dongyal Rinpoche traveled to northern India where he entered the monastic school of the Nyingma Monastery at Tso Pema, Rewalsar, on the banks of one of the holy lakes of Guru Padmasambhava. In 1967 he went to Sanskrit University, where he received B.A. and M.A. degrees in Buddhist Studies. In 1978 he was enthroned by H. H. Dudjom Rinpoche as Abbot of the Wish-fulfilling Nyingmapa Institute in Kathmandu, Nepal, where he taught Buddhist philosophy and literature for about three years. In 1981, at the request of H. H. Dudjom Rinpoche, he was appointed as Abbot of the Dorje Nyingpo Center in Paris, France. He continued to work closely with His Holiness until His Holiness passed away in 1987. Khenpo Tsewang Dongyal Rinpoche has taught in India, Nepal, Canada,

Russia, Puerto Rico, and throughout the United States. He has published books of poetry, Buddhist philosophy, and the early history of Tibetan Buddhism.

In 1985 Khenchen Palden Sherab and Khenpo Tsewang Dongyal founded Dharma Samudra, a nonprofit publishing organization, which began by publishing a Tibetan edition of eleven volumes of the hidden treasure teachings revealed by Tsasum Lingpa in the seventeenth century. The Rinpoches had worked for many years to gather these texts.

In 1988 they founded Padmasambhava Buddhist Center, which is incorporated as an international, nonprofit religious organization. Based at Padma Samye Ling, a monastery and retreat center in upstate New York, PBC includes over twenty local centers in the United States, Puerto Rico, and Russia. In 1996 the Venerable Khenpos completed building Padma Samye Chökhor Ling Monastery in Sarnath, India, where Buddha Shakyamuni gave his first teaching. Just a five-minute walk away, the Rinpoches established Orgyen Samye Chökhor Ling Nunnery in 2003, reflecting their commitment to equal opportunities for male and female students to study and practice. 2004 brought the fulfillment of a long-held vision: the consecration of the Great Miracle Stupa, Padma Samye Jetavan, in Shravasti, India. The new stupa rises in the vicinity of the original, ancient Miracle Stupa, first built to commemorate the miracles which Shakyamuni Buddha displayed at Jetavan Grove, and which had long ago been reduced to ruins. The new stupa is intended to last for a thousand years, radiating the energy of love and compassion to all beings.

The Venerable Khenpos often travel together and maintain schedules that include yearly visits to their centers, where they give teachings, empowerments, and individual meditation instruction. At the present time, they have jointly published the following works in English: *The Light of the Dharma, Prajnaparamita, Ceaseless Echoes of the Great Silence, Door to Inconceivable Wisdom and Compassion,* and *The Lion's Gaze.*

These works, including the present one, consist of their lectures given at the Padmasambhava Buddhist Centers around the world. Their individual published works include Khenchen Rinpoche's extensive commentary on "The Praise to the Twenty-One Taras," *The Smile of Sun and Moon,* and Khenpo Tsewang Rinpoche's epic poetic homage to Guru Padmasambhava, *Praise to the Lotus Born.*

Michael White

Traditional diagram of shamatha meditation practice,
illustrating the nine stages of mental development

Taming the Mind

Dharma is a Sanskrit word with ten different meanings. In the context of the Buddha's teachings, the dharma is what removes ignorance and reveals wisdom. By practicing the dharma we can bring out our innate wisdom and develop harmonious relationships with everyone.

Like all sentient beings in this world, we have problems and fears. If we try to find the cause of our unhappiness, we may think that there are various things and people in the world that cause our suffering, but this is not so. The external factors that bring sorrow at one time can bring joy at another time. We have to look inward to find the source of our problems. Everything we experience, whether pleasant or unpleasant, is the result of causes and conditions related to our state of mind.

The mind produces all our experiences and perceptions. When we tame the mind so that it rests calmly and clearly, then all our experiences are open and relaxed. When the mind is peaceful, then simultaneously the speech and body become peaceful. But if the mind is uncontrolled, then our words and actions are also out of control. Until we tame the mind, experiences of joy do not last more than a short time, no matter how many external supports we use. It is only by taming the mind that we can truly understand ourselves and others and find ultimate peace and joy.

People do many things in this life to become famous, rich, or successful. These things may provide momentary excitement, but they will not bring lasting happiness. For example, when you die you have to leave your wealth and power behind. No matter how famous you have been, sooner or later you are forgotten. Fame is like a thunderbolt that makes a loud noise but soon becomes silent. This lifetime is very precious because of the unique opportunity we now have to practice the dharma, to remove our ignorance and reveal our inner wisdom. If we do this, it will definitely benefit ourselves and others in this and future lives.

Dharma practice means taming the mind so that its true nature or essence is revealed. When you tame your mind, you find joy in this life and guidance for the bardo state after death. Controlling the mind brings peace and confidence and the ability to act with authority to accomplish your goals.

An important point about disciplining the mind is that it is something that we must do for ourselves. We cannot depend on someone else to do it for us. Buddha Shakyamuni taught that you are your own protector and savior. It is through controlling the mind that you will achieve realization and develop inner wisdom.

Taming the mind does not mean eliminating outer objects or suppressing inner thoughts. It means revealing and maintaining the natural state of the mind. Taming the mind has nothing to do with cultivating certain thoughts; it is simply keeping the mind in its fundamental state, where its clarity and wisdom are revealed. The true nature of the mind is calm and clear and full of compassion and love and wisdom.

We do not always experience the mind in this way because ignorance obscures our awareness of the mind's true nature. However, the wisdom nature is always there, and it can shine through and guide us in our lives. Even foolish people have wisdom and can exhibit beautiful qualities because this basic goodness is found equally in all beings. Not only human beings, but all sentient beings have the same nature and potential for enlightenment. The problem is that temporary obscurations cover and distort the essential nature of the mind. When we completely remove the ignorance and reveal the mind's true nature, we are enlightened.

It is important to remember that our true nature is only temporarily hidden. When we know that, we can work with courage and joy to remove the ignorance and let the essence of the mind shine forth. It is important for our diligence to be based on a joyful attitude, because without joyful effort we cannot reveal this true nature.

We need to exert ourselves now because this opportunity will not last forever. We must remember impermanence and the changing stages of life and death. Thinking about death and impermanence is often unpleasant — we usually do not like to acknowledge that everything, including ourselves, is subject to the law of incessant change. But change has good aspects as well, because without change there is no growth or improvement. With the right techniques, skills, and effort, we can learn and make positive changes. By understanding impermanence and causality we can work toward enlightenment and make the most of this human life.

As sentient beings we are constantly searching outside ourselves for happiness; but external causes of happiness never last. Eventually the happiness turns into suffering. After the suffering more happiness may arise, but we never seem to rest in ultimate peace. By reading history or by examining our own experiences we can see that external conditions never bring permanent joy.

This means that we have been looking in the wrong place, like thirsty people digging for water in rocky ground. They know water comes from the earth, so they dig and dig, but they are digging in the wrong place. Likewise, we should not look outward for the source of peace and happiness; it can only be found by looking inward and experiencing the natural state of the mind. The nature of the mind is not hollow or blank; it is profound and blissful and full of wonderful qualities. The mind is the source of both worldly existence and enlightenment, samsara and nirvana. Everything needed to find liberation from suffering is contained within the mind.

The teachings of dzogchen, "the great perfection," are the highest teachings of Buddha Shakyamuni and Guru Padmasambhava. These teachings have been passed down to us through the Nyingma lineage of Tibetan Buddhism. In the area where I was born in eastern Tibet, before the Chinese invaded, there was a famous dzogchen master who would travel from village to village and give teachings. His techniques were quite renowned. After teaching the foundation practices he would tell his students, "Now, it is your responsibility to find your own mind. Go out and find your mind and bring it back to me." Even if the students wanted to stay with him, he would not let them. He insisted they go off for at least three days to find their mind.

So, they went off in various directions; some went to the mountains and some went to the rivers. Many of his students thought they had to bring something back. One devoted student found some nice stones near a big river, and among the stones he found one particularly attractive white stone. He brought the rock back and told the master that he had found a stone that represented his mind. When the dzogchen master saw the stone, he grabbed the student by the collar and shouted, "What are you talking about? Are you crazy?" The student felt frightened and confused, and the master said, "This rock is not your mind; your mind is what is upset." For the first time the student gained some realization about the mind. Later, this student became a famous master.

Merely understanding the mind is not enough. Recognizing it as the source of happiness and suffering is good, but great results come only from looking inward and meditating on the nature of the mind. Once you recognize its nature, then you need to meditate with joyful effort. Joyful meditation will actualize the true nature of the mind, and maintaining the mind in this natural state will bring enlightenment. This type of meditation reveals the innermost, profound wisdom that is inherent in the mind.

Meditation can transform your body into wisdom light, into what is known as the rainbow body of wisdom. Many masters in the history of the Nyingma lineage have achieved this, as can anyone who practices these methods of meditation. The wisdom aspect of our nature exists at all times in each of us. You have always had this nature and it can be revealed through meditation. When you maintain the mind in its natural state, wonderful qualities shine out like light from the sun. Among these qualities are limitless compassion, limitless loving-kindness, and limitless wisdom.

To achieve this result as quickly as possible, people do meditation retreats. Among the Tibetan Buddhist schools, the Nyingma and Kagyu schools put great emphasis on retreat practice, both group retreats and individual retreats. Retreats are done in different ways for different lengths of time. The most popular are the three-day and the three-month retreats, but there are also three-year retreats. When people do three months or more, the main practice is to experience inner wisdom by maintaining the mind in its natural state. Other practices focus on doing prostrations, on developing loving-kindness and compassion, and on developing pure perception by visualizing a wisdom body and reciting mantras.

The purpose of retreat practice is to dedicate all activity to the practice of the dharma. During retreats the practitioners try to refrain from following their regular thoughts. The mind is maintained in the natural state, the speech is transformed into mantra, and the body is transformed into the wisdom body.

There is a famous story about two brothers who decided to go on retreat for three years. One of them, Drukpa Kunlek, was known as a crazy yogi. When they agreed to go on retreat, Drukpa Kunlek emphasized that they should stay in their retreat cabins for three years. He told his brother, "If you leave your retreat cabin, I will not stay any longer. As soon as you break the retreat, I am leaving too." His brother replied, "What are you saying? We are going on retreat, and that means we are not going to do anything else. Are you crazy?" Even his brother thought Drukpa Kunlek was a little bit crazy.

They were on retreat in two different cabins. The more conventional brother was the head of a monastery and he had many students and responsibilities. During the first week of the retreat, he thought about his

5

monastic duties and all the people involved in his work. He also designed a new building and did a lot of planning.

While the abbot was having all these thoughts, Drukpa Kunlek suddenly came out of his cabin and started laughing and shouting, "You broke retreat. I am not going to stay here because you broke the rules." The abbot replied, "How have I broken the rules? I never went out. I am still in retreat." Drukpa Kunlek was a great yogi who could read his brother's mind, and he said, "You went out of retreat when you were planning all those things for your monastery. Your mind has been all over the place. If the mind is traveling, there is no point in keeping the body in a cage. I'm leaving." Perhaps Drukpa Kunlek was acting crazily, but he understood that the real meaning of retreat is to maintain the mind in its natural state.

All the levels of the teachings by Buddha Shakyamuni are dedicated to subduing the mind and bringing out inner wisdom. Once we are able to tame our wild thoughts, then everlasting inner peace and joy will manifest. This is not a fairy tale — this can be demonstrated by personal experience. Once you have this realization, your mind will be unshakable like a mountain, always calm and peaceful.

Shakyamuni Buddha

The Causes and Conditions
of the Mind

Meditation practice reveals our true nature as being totally perfect and complete. However, at present, in an illusory and temporary way, we are incomplete. Although we have many good qualities, we also have many obstacles.

In order to reveal this completeness, the most important things to work with are the body, speech, and mind. In Buddhism, these three aspects are called the three doors. Along with the three doors, we cling to other dualistic labels like "he" and "she" and "I" and "you." Of all our concepts, the notions of having body, speech, and mind are always with us, so if we can make their activities positive, then we are performing dharmic activity. If we do not have the ability to make our body, speech, and mind positive, then we are in either a neutral or a negative state.

It is very important to tame the mind because it is the basis for speech and action. Buddha Shakyamuni and many Buddhist masters have said that the mind is like a king and the body and speech are like servants. We do not have to believe this just because the Buddha taught it; we can test it in our own experience. If the mind accepts something, then the body and speech follow. If the mind is not satisfied, no matter how nice it looks on the outside, the body and speech will refuse it.

Since mindfulness supports what is positive, we should try to be mindful in all our activities. Along with mindfulness, we should always try to be honest and compassionate and helpful to others. If we direct our mind, along with our body and speech, in a positive direction, we will definitely become more peaceful, clear, and relaxed.

In our present state we are continually thinking about "me" and "mine." When we observe this thinking about "me," we see that it is just a way in which we grasp and hold on to the idea of a self.

What is the relationship between the self and the body? If we do not investigate at all or if we just look at the surface, we might say that the feeling of having a self seems to rely on the body, and at the same time, the body seems to rely on the sense of the self. But if we analyze carefully, these two things are totally different. The body is not "I" and "I" is not the body. The body is made of the five elements: earth, water, fire, wind, and space. Also, we have the five aggregates of form, feeling, perception, mental formations, and consciousness. The form aggregate refers to the physical body and the other aggregates are part of the mind. But all of the elements and the aggregates are different from the self, and the self is different from them.

The "I" exists when we start to form attachments; the "I" is nothing other than the grasping itself. As for what is doing the grasping, it is the mind. Since all the notions of a grasping self are developed by the mind, the mind is the most important thing to understand.

On the gross level it seems as if the mind relies upon the body. Without investigating, the body looks more stable than the mind. For example, when you get sick, the physical pain affects your mind so that you feel unhappy. When your body becomes more comfortable, then you feel better mentally as well. However, if you look deeper with your inner wisdom, you can tell that the mind does not rely on the body; it is the body that relies on the mind. The body is merely temporary and dependent upon the mind. The mind is like the ground; it is more vast and subtle than the body.

The mind is also more subtle than the speech. Speech is developed by the body and the mind, but mainly by the body. According to the Buddhist point of view, there are 1,072 principal nerves or channels that extend throughout the body, and all of them are filled with wind. The way speech develops is that first you have a thought, which travels with the wind. The wind pushes and makes vibrations in the channels and then speech is formed. It is possible to touch the body but it is not possible to touch sound. Speech is not the body, and yet it is also not the mind.

To see how vast and subtle the mind is, we can look at the continuity of our thoughts. For example, the present thought developed from the thought of the previous instant. Thoughts continue from the previous minute, the previous hour, from today, yesterday, and so on.

It is important to investigate whether or not the present thought has a cause. The present thought is a result, and every result must have a cause. Everything that we see or hear or touch has causes and conditions. Our past thoughts influence our present thoughts. The mind does not come from something permanent; the mind is changing and moving every instant. If the mind were permanent, we would not be thinking at this moment, because permanent means unchanging. But thoughts change constantly. For example, as these words change, your mind changes accordingly. It never stays the same.

There are thousands of instants of thoughts; each follows the other continuously like a river. The present thought is the result of the last thought, which was the result of the thought before that, and so on. For example, where does the consciousness come from at nine o'clock? It is a result of the consciousness at eight o'clock. The mind at eight o'clock came from the mind at seven o'clock, which came from the mind at six o'clock, and so forth.

In the same way, the thoughts we have today came from our thoughts yesterday. And yesterday's consciousness came from the day before yesterday. And this month's consciousness came from last month, and this year's consciousness came from last year. Investigating in this way, you can see that your consciousness goes back to the day you were born.

Your sense of identity comes from your consciousness as an infant, starting when you were so small that your mother could carry you in one hand. How did that baby develop? It came from your mother's womb;

your body developed from the two elements of your parents. But those two elements could not develop a baby if there were no consciousness. When your consciousness was trapped between those two elements, that was your conception, and gradually you were formed. Your consciousness was the cause, and the dominant condition was the two elements of your parents. When a cause and certain conditions occur perfectly at the right time, then a specific result develops.

The consciousness that was trapped between the two elements of your parents came from the bardo, or intermediate state. Your consciousness in the bardo state came from your consciousness at death in your last life. The consciousness at death in your last life can be traced back to your consciousness at birth in that life. And that birth's consciousness goes back and back and back to beginningless time.

This is how you can trace your mind. Your present mind has a cause and it has conditions, and it will continue without interruption until you attain enlightenment. The continuation of consciousness through different stages is what Buddhists call past and future lives. Even though at this moment you do not remember your past lifetimes, or you do not understand how you were conceived in your mother's womb, there is definitely a continuation. You have come here now, and you will go on continuously in the future. It is similar to seeing a flowing river. Since the river has arrived at this point, you know it must be continuous. Even though you cannot see its source, you know that the river has come from somewhere and will continue to go somewhere. You have come from the past, from beginningless time. Now you are here, and your consciousness will continue tomorrow, the day after tomorrow, next week, next month, and next year.

It is very important to understand the way causes and conditions work because this understanding brings inner wisdom. The cause of the body is the elements and the cause of consciousness is consciousness itself. Whatever results will be similar to the causes and conditions that produced it. For example, if we plant a seed of wheat, we will grow wheat, not corn or soybeans. Similarly, human beings give birth to human beings, not donkeys or elephants.

Buddha Shakyamuni taught extensively about cause and result. In one sutra he taught by using the example of rice growing in a field. The Buddha said to a farmer, "Where does a grain of rice come from? Each grain of rice comes from the rice that you planted the year before. It did not develop from a permanent cause or from no cause; it developed from a similar cause and certain conditions. Last year's rice also had a similar cause, and it goes back to beginningless time. Nobody can tell exactly where the first grain of rice came from. Also, a cause must be complete to produce an effect; it cannot be faulty or damaged. If this grain of rice does not encounter any major obstacles, it will go on endlessly in the future. The same cause will bring the same results again and again. But if we cook this rice and eat it, that will cut the continuity of the results." Similarly, it is very important for us to understand how cause and effect relate to the mind — to know how the mind develops, what it is like now, and how far it will go.

One day all of us will have to go through the stage of death; we have done it before and we will do it again. Nobody can ignore or run away from death. When we feel afraid to die it is because we do not understand the nature of death. Death is the separation of the body from consciousness; that is all. The body developed from the five elements and it will dissolve back into the elements, but consciousness did not develop from the elements. Since the mind is different from the elements, it will flow on continuously.

We might doubt the existence of past and future lives, because we think nothing exists beyond what we can perceive with our senses. But actually, we are uncertain.

What happens after death, according to the Buddhist teachings, is that the body, the form aggregate, does not continue, but the other four aggregates of feeling, perception, mental formations, and consciousness continue. In terms of consciousness, the habitual tendencies connected with the five sense consciousnesses, and the mental consciousness, the emotional consciousness, and the alaya consciousness travel to the next life. The alaya is the subconscious mind that is mixed with karmic habitual tendencies. This deepest part of consciousness goes on to the next life.

Habitual tendencies are one part of karma. After people die they no longer have the eye, ear, nose, tongue, and body consciousnesses. Although the five sense consciousnesses are not active at that point, their habitual patterns continue. It is the same as when you are dreaming; your five senses are not functioning, but you still perceive yourself seeing and hearing and talking. Actually, those things are not happening; they are only habitual perceptions. Similarly, in the bardo state there is no sensory activity, only habitual tendencies. In that way the alaya and the habitual patterns go together to the next life.

It is the conscious mind that reincarnates. One could say that the mind travels to the next stage, and when it encounters the necessary conditions, there is rebirth. This is not the reincarnation of a truly existing, permanent mind, because the nature of the mind is emptiness. In fact, it is only because of emptiness that it is possible to be reborn. If the mind were permanent, it could not change. We are reborn due to ignorance, and once the ignorance is removed through the realization of emptiness, we are not forced to reincarnate. People who realize the nature of the mind are liberated and do not reincarnate by the power of karma.

It is similar to having a large piece of gold but not recognizing what it is. If you do not know its worth, then what is the benefit of having it? But if you recognize that it is gold, then you will be wealthy. Likewise, if you neurotically cling to things as being solid and real, then the natural state is not self-liberating. The impetus of current habits will continue to carry your consciousness to rebirth after rebirth.

Just knowing about emptiness is not enough to stop reincarnation.

Mere intellectual understanding is not realization. According to Buddhism, understanding and realization are different. We may understand something, but we have to experience it to gain realization. For example, if we look at a map we can know something about the place we are going, but it does not mean that we are there. If we go there, we will experience something quite different from what is on the map. However, learning from a map is very helpful. Similarly, understanding emptiness is the first stage of realizing the true nature of the mind.

Emptiness is not the cause of rebirth; habitual, dualistic grasping causes rebirth. At the same time, emptiness is what makes it possible for things to change. Reincarnation does not mean that the mind does not change; without change there is no birth. For instance, when we plant a flower, it is changing, step-by-step, moment by moment. The seed becomes a sprout, and the sprout continues to change until it becomes a flower. Or consider a building — even if we cannot see it with our eyes, it has been subtly changing ever since it was built. It is the same way with each of us — our bodies and thoughts are changing in each moment. In every moment we have the opportunity to let go of our habitual clinging.

Ignorance blocks our vision in many ways. For example, if someone asks us where the mind came from or where it will go in the future, or how long we will live on this earth, we do not know the answers. Ignorance has covered up wisdom to the extent that we do not even understand the way things work at the relative level of cause and effect. Buddha Shakyamuni said that sentient beings are wandering in darkness, unable to see beyond what they can feel.

Ignorance also obscures the mind's enlightened qualities. One way that ignorance obscures the wisdom mind is through negative emotions like anger, jealousy, and desire, which keep the mind from remaining in the natural state. When we are under the control of negative emotions, we simply cannot have a peaceful state of mind. We find ourselves worried and uneasy, floating in an ocean of ignorance, where we are tossed about by waves of resentment, fear and attachment.

It is important to remember that ignorance can be removed; it is not the fundamental nature of the mind. If we understand the causes and effects of ignorance and wisdom, we can work to remove confusion and bring out the inherent enlightened qualities.

HUNG, Sanskrit seed syllable of primordial mind
(calligraphy by Khenchen Palden Sherab Rinpoche)

The Primordial Nature

As human beings we operate on the level of confused relative appearances, making distinctions and perceiving things as good or bad, helpful or harmful, true or false. But all these concepts and judgments come from our imagination. The relative truth of the way things appear may be accurate in our current situation, but it is not the absolute truth of the way things really are.

In the natural state of reality, all things are equal. The natural state is beyond any ideas we may have and even beyond our imagination. From the perspective of the natural state, all our plans and actions are merely imaginary, like the play of children that has nothing to do with reality. Once we understand the true nature of the relative level, then we can reach the absolute level, which is enlightenment. When we fully realize the wisdom of self-born awareness, we become buddhas who are liberated in the state of nirvana.

In normal awareness we operate on the basis of habits. But continuing to follow habitual patterns will not lead to enlightenment; we will only stay the same and never achieve higher understanding. Our present mind is like a nest constructed of subtle and gross thoughts. We think in terms of subjects and objects, inside and outside. We are constantly judging people and situations, seeing them as beautiful or ugly, pleasant or unpleasant, right or wrong.

Who is making all these decisions and judgments? We might say, "I did that, I felt that." But really, what is this "I"? Where is it? Who is doing all the analyzing and discriminating? To find out, we must look at the mind. It is the mind that does the analyzing and discriminating.

If we look carefully at the mind, we begin to understand its nature. When we look for the mind, we discover how difficult it is to find. We cannot put it in our hands. We cannot see it or its nature. The mind is a vast emptiness called shunyata, or great emptiness. The emptiness nature does not mean that it is blank or a black hole. The mind has many beautiful qualities, like clarity and wisdom, yet these qualities are inseparable from emptiness.

Emptiness is not the same as nonexistence, which is symbolized in Buddhist philosophy by impossibilities like the horns of a rabbit or the child of a barren woman. The reality of the mind is emptiness, yet the mind reflects and radiates awareness in every direction. In the dzogchen teachings Buddha Shakyamuni taught that the nature of the mind is clarity and vastness, and that it is always enlightened. It is more open than space, clearer than crystal, brighter than the sun. However, our mind is usually very active and full of confused thoughts. If we sit and look at the mind for just one minute, we can see it wandering in different directions, roaming around like a drunken elephant or jumping like a restless monkey from tree to tree. The relative nature of the mind is continuously arising mental activity.

Different types of outer objects provoke different mental reactions. All our reactions can be summarized in three main categories: feelings of happiness, feelings of suffering, and neutral feelings. Once you have experienced a feeling of happiness, then you desire to have a similar experience, then a third and a fourth and a fifth and a sixth. There is no end to this and no satisfaction. You simply want more and more, and you end up striving to attain it again and again. This is attachment. Then, inevitably there will be times when you experience the opposite of happiness. Suffering and negative emotions arise and you experience anger over the fact that something is disturbing your happiness. This also has no end; it repeats itself over and over. When you are attached to pleasant feelings, you simultaneously build up other attachments. When you experience happiness, it can lead to pride or jealousy at the same time. All thoughts and feelings are developed through a system of cause and effect.

The effect of one cause becomes the cause of the next effect, and so on.

Experiences and feelings come from the mind. Our confused experiences will disappear when we maintain the mind in the natural state. Enlightenment is simply maintaining the mind in its own clarity and emptiness. It is similar to muddy water becoming clear when it is left alone. Nothing special is needed to reveal the mind's true nature; one simply remains in the natural state. There is nothing to do but sit and relax.

When we are active, we generate more thoughts and find ourselves caught in an endless circle of thinking and feeling. When we meditate we stop turning this wheel. From the perspective of the natural state we can see that our world is created by our thoughts. Everything that we know, simply by virtue of our knowing it, is created by the mind. For example, in our everyday life we follow various standards of conduct. Someone might say that a certain way of behaving is not appropriate; this simply means that the behavior is not correct according to that person's habitual thinking. All rules of conduct are merely creations of people's minds.

Conceptual thinking operates on the basis of habitual patterns. The habits that you repeat circle back on you again and again and again. Whatever habits are learned in this lifetime will be reflected in future lifetimes; they are maintained within the mind. Whatever felt comfortable when you were a child formed into habitual patterns that continue now that you are grown. The habits you establish in your mind are reflected in your behavior. In Buddhism this is known as the law of karmic cause and effect.

There are different levels to the mind. We have five aspects of consciousness: the eye consciousness, the ear consciousness, the nose consciousness, the tongue consciousness, and the body consciousness. The five sense consciousnesses are related to the five sense organs; they do nothing more than take in the five kinds of perceptions.

Behind the senses we have the mental consciousness. The mental consciousness analyzes the perceptions of the senses. For example, the eye consciousness brings what it sees to the mind, and the mind analyzes it and discriminates in terms of good, bad, or neutral. It does the same thing with perceptions of the ear, nose, tongue, and body. The mind consciousness also analyzes perceptions in relation to the past, present and future.

The level of mind where the habits are stored is known as the *alaya*, or the subconscious. All of our activities and states of mind rely on this subconscious storehouse, which is very deep and subtle, like the ocean. All thoughts arise from and go back to this state. In deep sleep the six consciousnesses dissolve back into the alaya and you do not have dreams. In light sleep dreams begin to appear, and as you awaken, your thoughts manifest once again.

Behind the alaya is great emptiness, the true nature. Emptiness is the source of all mental activity, and all movements of the mind are pervaded by primordial awareness. The primordial nature of the mind is not separate from the relative phenomena we perceive right now. It is not the case that the primordial nature is good and the relative nature is bad. They are two sides of the nature of mind. If awareness is focused only on regular thoughts, we remain unaware of the primordial nature and this one-sidedness prevents understanding of the way things really are.

The true nature of mind is beyond conception, yet it is present in every object. The true nature is always there, but due to our temporary obscurations we do not recognize it. From the dzogchen perspective, samsara and nirvana are equal. We cannot reject one aspect and accept the other because both samsara and nirvana are manifestations of the true nature of awareness.

Buddha Shakyamuni taught that this world comes from the primordial nature. Whether we recognize the primordial nature or not, whether our actions are based on that understanding or not, we are never separated from primordial nature.

The primordial nature is beyond all concepts. It is the beginning of the mind and the end of the mind. We already have it; we do not need anything further. The Buddha and other great masters taught that there is nothing to acquire externally; it is only a matter of working to reveal what we already have. In the *Prajñaparamita Sutra* the Buddha taught that there is nothing to gain and nothing to lose. We already have enlightenment, but we have to realize it personally.

Although the primordial nature is inconceivable and insubstantial, it is not truly nonexistent. To find and experience its nature of clarity and emptiness you must look at the mind. The primordial nature is beyond conceptions; it cannot be explained. Emotions and other mental activities can be explained, but the primordial nature of the mind cannot be encompassed by words. Although you can say it is clarity and vastness, you cannot see it or touch it; it is beyond expression.

The primordial nature is described as the union of clear light and emptiness. Describing the true nature in words is like looking through a window and seeing the sky as square. The actual nature of the mind cannot be expressed since it is completely beyond concepts. All you can do is look at your own mind and experience its primordial nature. When you are able to maintain that state, you reach enlightenment.

There is a story told in Buddhist texts that shows how the mind operates in relation to nirvana and samsara. There was once a prince who lived in a beautiful palace. One night, while having a nightmare, he walked out of the palace and went to a different country where nobody knew him. Eventually, he forgot he was a prince. He worked hard at various jobs; he did not always have good food or clothes, and he suffered a lot. Then, one day he remembered that he was a prince who had lived in a palace. He remembered how to get back and he returned to his palace and became the prince again. Everyone was overjoyed and showed him great respect.

What was the difference in the prince when he was suffering in the world and when he was living in the palace? He was the same person

23

before and after he returned to his kingdom. Nothing was different except his recognition. When he recognized himself as a prince, he acted like a prince. That is the only difference.

In our case, we are known as human beings, and people who are enlightened are known as buddhas. The only difference between the buddhas and ourselves is that the buddhas are aware of their primordial nature while we have not yet come to this recognition. There is a story about this concerning Drukpa Kunlek, the crazy yogi mentioned earlier. One time he went to a temple in Lhasa where there is a famous statue of the Buddha. This statue is said to have been blessed by Buddha Shakyamuni himself. You may have seen photographs of this place; Tibetans try to go there on pilgrimage at least once in their lives. When people visit this statue they bring incense, make offerings, and do a lot of prostrations.

When Drukpa Kunlek went to the temple, he did not prostrate, but just stood there looking at the statue. The priest who took care of the shrine felt a little funny because Drukpa Kunlek was not showing the proper respect. After a while, Drukpa Kunlek composed a verse and then did prostrations. He said, "At the beginning of time, you and I were equal; there was no difference between us. You worked to recognize your nature and became enlightened. I did not recognize my nature and merely slept. Therefore, I will prostrate, not to you, but in recognition of your excellent endeavor."

The buddhas are not higher than us, and we are not lower than the buddhas; we are equal. The only difference is whether the buddha nature has been recognized. We have to work to experience that recognition, but once we recognize it we are the same as all the buddhas. There is no difference in the ground of our basic nature.

Whoever connects will destroy all peril and feeble situations.
The infallible three jewels, as lama, will never deceive.
From now on, from the depth of my heart,
I take refuge until I attain the heart of enlightenment.

Spontaneous poem by Khenchen Palden Sherab Rinpoche
(calligraphy by Khenpo Tsewang Dongyal Rinpoche)

Taking Refuge

The first step in practicing Buddhism, according to the three traditions of hinayana, mahayana, and vajrayana, is to take refuge. The seed or cause for taking refuge is a feeling of interest and closeness to the three objects of refuge: the Buddha, the dharma, and the sangha. On the outer level, the Buddha is the person who gave the teachings; he is the guide. The dharma is the teachings; it is a guidebook that describes where to go. The sangha are the beings who follow the path described by the dharma. There are different levels of the sangha — some members of the sangha are highly realized beings and some are beginners, but anyone who follows the Buddhist path is a member of the sangha. This is the outer meaning of taking refuge.

The three refuges also have an inner meaning related to the mind. The mind's primordial nature is totally pure, clear, and enlightened from beginningless time. One's own pure awareness is the primordial buddha. Buddha actually means the perfect understanding that is free from all deluded and dualistic thinking. This is the absolute buddha.

Maintaining the qualities of the primordial nature and radiating them to all sentient beings is the inner meaning of taking refuge in the absolute dharma. *Dharma* is a Sanskrit word that can be translated as "protection." Practicing the dharma protects the mind from delusion and duality. The mind contains tremendous, vast qualities that cannot be put into words. The primordial nature of the mind includes a completely nonviolent attitude of infinite loving-kindness and infinite compassion toward all beings, and these qualities are known as the dharma.

The inner sangha is also contained within the mind. *Sangha* is a Sanskrit word meaning "inseparable." This refers to the inseparability of clarity and emptiness as the true nature of the mind. These qualities are always present as the unity of skillful means and wisdom. Clarity and emptiness are always present, and that is the meaning of the absolute sangha.

Anyone can take refuge; it is open to everyone who has joyful interest and devotion toward the Buddha, the dharma, and the sangha. As a Buddhist, you continue to take refuge on both outer and inner levels until you come to a full realization of primordial awareness. When you have achieved enlightenment, then you do not have to take refuge any longer; instead you become an object of refuge.

The refuge ceremony conveys the lineage blessings of Buddha Shakyamuni, the dharma, and the sangha. When taking the refuge vow, a person should have the pure motivation of doing it for the sake of all sentient beings. During the ceremony, the participants meditate on the historical buddha, Buddha Shakyamuni, as the representation of enlightenment. They visualize him in the sky in front of them as a real, living buddha who is radiating wisdom light in every direction. He is surrounded by many realized beings, such as bodhisattvas and arhats and the buddhas of the three times. All of them are smiling and radiating rainbow light of wisdom and blessings.

The aim of taking refuge is to remove the dark ignorance of sentient beings and to reveal their true awareness. To affirm this, the teacher and students chant three times: "I take refuge in the Buddha, the dharma, and the sangha until I become enlightened. I am doing this for the benefit of all sentient beings." When the chant is repeated for the third time, the students visualize wisdom light radiating from the objects of refuge and entering their hearts. At that moment the teacher snaps his fingers and the students receive the lineage blessings. Then, each student receives a dharma name, and a little piece of their hair is cut off. The piece of hair is an offering to the Buddha, the dharma, the sangha, and the teacher. This indicates the change from being an ordinary person to being a member of the Buddhist sangha.

The Tibetan script for discipline, concentration, and wisdom –
tsultrim, ting'dzin, and sherab — *by Khenpo Tsewang Dongyal Rinpoche*

Training in Discipline, Concentration, and Wisdom

The primordial nature of the mind is filled with inherent qualities of bliss, compassion, and wisdom. It is always peaceful and fresh. In order to bring out these inner qualities, Buddha Shakyamuni taught the three techniques of discipline, concentration, and wisdom.

According to the Buddhist teachings, discipline is not like following orders or being forced to do something; discipline means to relate fully with your own mind. In order to uncover our true nature we need to discipline our body, we need to discipline our speech, and we need to discipline our mind. Discipline is the first stage of cleaning up and preparing for further developments. It is like clearing the ground — if we want to erect a beautiful building, we need to clear the surface first.

Not only in practicing the dharma, but also in the ordinary world, we need to pay careful attention to what we are doing. Just as good planning is important in ordinary activities, discipline is important in practicing the dharma. Discipline should be accompanied by mindfulness, careful attention, and joyful effort.

With good discipline as the ground, the next step is to develop concentration. It is not enough to be disciplined and well prepared for future developments; to get good results we also need concentration. Concentration is directly related to our discursive thoughts; until we develop good concentration we will remain on the surface of the mind without discovering its deeper wisdom.

You know how your mind is working right now without needing to ask someone else. You can simply ask yourself; you already know. For example, all day your thoughts have been running on and on, not stopping for even a minute. Your thoughts continue from the time you wake

31

up until the time you go to sleep. Since your body does not have the energy to keep going, you need to sleep, but even when you are dreaming your mind is still active. When you wake up in the morning, even if your body does not want to get up, your mind makes it go in different directions. Your mind also directs your speech to say various things, sometimes nice and sometimes not so nice. Your body and speech act according to the direction of your mind.

To discipline your mind and have concentration you need to become your own teacher. A skillful teacher can give guidelines and instructions to assist you, but real discipline and concentration must come from yourself. External supports or forces cannot subdue your mind and bring good concentration. For example, in this country you see the police carrying pistols and sticks, but there continues to be violence, which shows that external force cannot do all that much. If you become your own teacher and your own law, that will be worth more than a million police surrounding you.

To develop discipline and concentration requires continual practice with joyous effort. If you have been practicing with concentration for a few days or a few weeks, that will bring some results, but it will not bring great results. I am not saying that meditating for one day or one week will not help you; it will help you, but not a lot. For example, if you want to walk from here to a distant town, it is too much to think that you will arrive there by taking three steps. You will be a little bit closer, but you cannot reach your destination in three steps. However, if you continue with joyful effort and courage, you will get closer and closer to your goal.

If you have the time to practice meditation for one year without any major obstacles, that will definitely bring good results. You probably will not reach enlightenment after a year, but you will certainly have more mastery over your mind. If you meditate for two years, the results will be doubled or even tripled. If you continue to meditate for five or ten years, you will have more control of your mind and be able

32

to reveal more of its inner qualities.

When you meditate with concentration, there are three particular experiences that arise: bliss, clarity, and nonthought. Sometimes you feel great joy, sometimes your mind is very clear, and sometimes there is complete equanimity. To experience these you do not need to meditate for a long time, although for a beginner these experiences will not last long because of the limited ability of a beginner's meditation.

The experience of meditative bliss is greater than ordinary worldly happiness. Sometimes when you are meditating, a feeling of blissfulness suddenly arises from the subtle state of your mind and pervades your entire body. This bliss is healthy and brings out your inner qualities. Some people use drugs to induce blissfulness and visions, but drugs are external supports that cannot bring lasting happiness. The bliss experienced in meditation can last for many days, according to your ability to meditate. When you experience this kind of bliss, on the outside you might look very poor, but inside you remain very joyful.

The second main experience in meditation is clarity. Sometimes while meditating you can suddenly feel that your mind is very clear and bright. Even if you are meditating in the dark, you do not feel heavy or tired. Sometimes your body feels very light and your mind is very clear, and many kinds of reflections appear. Clarity brings great wisdom and the ability to read other people's minds, as well as to see your own past and future lives.

The third main experience is nonthought, or a state of equanimity without distractions. Beginners can also experience this. Nonthought is more settled than the experiences of bliss and clarity. If you have thoughts, they suddenly dissolve and you can remain continuously in meditation. As your ability to meditate develops, your mind becomes more and more settled, so that you can meditate for one hour or one week or one month without being distracted by thoughts. You simply remain in the natural state for as long as you want.

Bliss, clarity, and nonthought are the main qualities of concentration. However, it is important not to be attached to them or concerned about whether they arise or not; one should simply continue to practice.

Along with discipline and concentration we also need wisdom. The nature of wisdom is emptiness-clarity; it is always fresh and complete and free from all confused thinking. Primordial wisdom is the only thing that can dispel the darkness of ignorance, so it is compared to the light of the sun. Primordial wisdom is the cause of enlightenment, or one could say that primordial wisdom itself is enlightenment.

Wisdom is not something we can obtain from outside ourselves; it has been with us from beginningless time. This enlightened nature pervades every sentient being equally. It is not the case that only the Buddha has this nature; it exists in every mind. Although ignorance and obscurations cover our wisdom, the primordial nature is always radiating. For example, we know in a general way what is good for us and what is bad for us. This is the power of the primordial wisdom, radiating through the heaviness of ignorance.

However, for wisdom to manifest we have to work to bring it out. The discovery of wisdom requires relating with your mind by having discipline and concentration. In the beginning of dharma practice it is important to know that the mind is the most important thing to work with, and the best ways to work with it are through discipline, concentration, and wisdom. By practicing these three techniques, enlightenment is right here with us.

*Thousand-arm form of Avalokiteshvara (Chenrezig in Tibetan),
buddha of compassion*

Cultivating Bodhichitta

It is important to realize that enlightenment is totally dependent upon your own effort. It is not something that a teacher can give you or that you can find outside yourself. Your mind has an enlightened nature which can only manifest by your own effort and actions. You have the natural capacity to be enlightened, and it is in your hands whether or not you actualize this opportunity.

The best way to actualize enlightenment is to develop bodhichitta. *Bodhichitta* is a Sanskrit word; *bodhi* means "enlightenment" and *chitta* means "mind" or "thought." When you develop the thought of enlightenment, you are training your mind so that you will be able to truly benefit other beings. Bodhichitta can be understood in two ways, as relative and absolute. Relative bodhichitta is the actual manifestation of loving-kindness and compassion for all beings. Absolute bodhichitta is the realization of emptiness as the profound true nature of reality. Some people start meditating on love and compassion and then come to an understanding of emptiness. Other people meditate on emptiness and, by that, gain an understanding of love and compassion. Both aspects of bodhichitta are part of the enlightened nature of the mind.

Bodhichitta is very precious and important; if you do not have bodhichitta, no matter what other techniques you use, you will never attain enlightenment. When Buddha Shakyamuni gave teachings to the king of the nagas, he said, "Great naga king, if you have just one thing, that will be enough to attain enlightenment." When the naga king asked what that might be, the Buddha replied, "It is bodhichitta." Whenever you practice any form of meditation or perform any beneficial activity, you should invest these practices with bodhichitta so that they will lead to enlightenment.

The thought of enlightenment is the intention to benefit all sentient beings, without any concern for your own welfare. When you practice according to the bodhisattva's motivation, you dedicate all your practice and activities for others; you focus on opening your heart to them without any attachment to yourself. If you think, "I want to practice to get rid of my emotional problems and be happy," that attitude is not bodhichitta. If you work for yourself alone, thinking, "I want to attain liberation," that is a very small liberation. If you work for the benefit of others, since your motivation and actions are much more vast, you reach "the great liberation," or *mahaparinirvana* in Sanskrit. Of course, you also become liberated, but you are working primarily for all sentient beings.

The root of bodhichitta is compassion. Compassion is feeling, deep in your heart, the suffering of others and wishing for them to be free from all pain. The root of compassion is loving-kindness, which is the feeling of wanting to replace suffering with happiness and peace. Having true love and compassion for everyone is the most precious practice of the dharma. Without this, your practice will remain superficial and never be deeply rooted in the true dharma.

The feelings of love should be extended to every sentient being, without partiality. Compassion should be directed toward all beings in all directions, not just to human beings or to certain beings in certain places. All beings existing in space, all those who are searching for happiness and joy, should be put under the umbrella of our compassion. At the present time our love and compassion are very limited. Our bodhichitta is so tiny that it looks like a small dot; it does not expand in all directions. However, bodhichitta can be developed; it is not outside the realm of our potential. Once it has been developed, this small dot of bodhichitta can expand to fill the entire universe.

Whenever we begin to learn something new it is difficult because we are not used to it, but if we train diligently then it becomes easy. Shantideva, the great meditation master and scholar, said that there is nothing that remains difficult once it becomes familiar. You can see this from your own experience. When you were a baby, so small that your mother could carry you in one hand, you did not even know how to eat or use the toilet. But now you are far beyond that and what you have learned has become easy.

Similarly, we can learn to develop bodhichitta. There are many examples of people, like the great masters of India and Tibet, who became familiar with the thought of enlightenment and accomplished it. For example, before Buddha Shakyamuni was enlightened he was just an ordinary person. In the Jataka Tales there are many stories about the ways he practiced bodhichitta before he became enlightened. Over the course of many lifetimes he dedicated his wealth and property, and even his life, for all beings. By working diligently to understand the true nature of the mind and by dedicating all his activities to others, he became enlightened. If we work at it, we can achieve the same result.

All sentient beings are equal in that all of us want happiness. To see this clearly, the Buddha said that you should use yourself as an example. Just as you do not want to be harmed, in the same way no one else wants to be harmed. If someone is hurting you, then you cannot be happy, and it is exactly the same with others. When you are suffering you want to remove whatever is bothering you; you do not want to keep the cause of your suffering for even one minute. Similarly, other sentient beings want to be free of problems and pain. When you practice bodhichitta you realize that all beings are equal in this way.

Relative bodhichitta can be divided into two types: these are called wishing bodhichitta and actualizing bodhichitta. The first is the intention to benefit others. As you begin to realize how much other beings suffer, you develop the wish to remove their misery and establish them in happiness. In the second stage, actualizing bodhichitta, you actually work to help others. After developing the intention, you must do whatever you can to help, in accordance with your capabilities. It is not easy to remove the suffering of all beings, but you can begin with those near you, and as you develop your abilities you can help more beings until eventually you are helping everyone.

To practice bodhichitta, you need to dedicate your efforts freely and openly without expecting anything in return. The more you meditate and practice bodhichitta, the more you feel that others are as dear as yourself, and eventually their welfare becomes even more important than your own. Buddha Shakyamuni told a story about putting another's welfare above one's own. One time a mother and her daughter needed to cross a big river that had no bridge or boats. They tried to swim across, but the currents were very strong, and when they reached the center of the river they were swept apart. As the mother was drowning she felt great compassion for her daughter and thought, "It is all right if I am carried away by this water, but I wish my daughter would survive." While having that loving intention she died. The daughter was thinking the same way: "It is all right if I drown, but I hope my mother will survive." At that very moment she also died. The Buddha said that because of their genuine thoughts of love and compassion, they were both immediately reborn in a higher god realm called the Brahma Realm.

In general, your state of mind right before you die is very important. At the moment just before death, even the smallest thought can change the direction of your rebirth. It is good to remember this when you are with people who are dying. It is important to let them die in peace, without stirring up their emotions. It definitely helps people if they die with peaceful thoughts. Further, if you can create thoughts of love and compassion in a person's heart just before their death, it will change their future life.

In his teachings, Buddha Shakyamuni praised the qualities of love and compassion not just once or twice, but again and again. He said if you practice true love and compassion for even one moment, it will bring enormous benefit, and if compassionate behavior becomes your way of life, it will lead directly to enlightenment.

"The Four Friends" or *"Harmonious Brothers,"* a traditional Buddhist tale

Loving-kindness

Once you know about the thought of enlightenment, the next step is to increase this type of awareness. As much as possible, you should work diligently to increase your motivation to attain enlightenment for the benefit of others. In your daily practice you can pray that those beings who have not yet generated bodhichitta may quickly do so, and that those beings, including yourself, who are already cultivating bodhichitta will increase it.

Compassion is based on loving-kindness. When you feel compassion for people and animals, even for just a few of them, it is because you love them. Once you have developed true loving-kindness you no longer act violently or hurt anyone. When your loving-kindness becomes immeasurable, you want all sentient beings to be happy and you treat all of them as your loved ones.

Typically, at the present time, we love only a few people — ourselves, our family, and our close friends. This limited notion of love is an ordinary emotion. The love between two people is part of the love and compassion we are talking about, but this form of love is based on attachment and clinging. The immeasurable love of bodhichitta is based on emptiness. Since infinite love is combined with equanimity, it is not an emotion.

In order to expand your love, take your own feelings as an example and apply that to others. Just as you want happiness and peace, all sentient beings want happiness and peace. No one wants to suffer; everyone wants to be happy. By practicing loving-kindness we can help others find the happiness and peace they desire.

Buddha Shakyamuni taught that of the one thousand buddhas of this aeon, three buddhas have already come and he is the fourth. The next supreme buddha of this aeon will be Maitreya, whose name means "loving-kindness." In the *Mahayana Maitreya Sutra,* Buddha Shakyamuni describes him, saying that Buddha Maitreya will become enlightened by practicing only one technique — loving-kindness. Since that will be the cause of his enlightenment, his name is Maitreya.

Practicing loving-kindness will increase our tolerance for difficult people and difficult situations, and eventually it will bring the result of enlightenment. At the present time we find it hard to practice patience; as soon as we hear criticism or someone says a few harsh words, we feel upset and want to react. It is difficult to be patient because we do not have enough love and compassion. When we find it hard to be patient, that is a sign that we need to develop more love. Similarly, when there are troubles between nations around the world or when family members have problems, it is because there is a lack of love and compassion. When a person has true love and compassion, patience will spontaneously be there.

When you generate bodhichitta, you will be happy about what you are doing. There are two reasons for this happiness: first, you are actualizing bodhichitta within yourself, and second, you are engaged in working for all beings. Among the many different thoughts you have every day, the thought of enlightenment is the most important. As you develop this thought and increase it to include all the sentient beings who are in need, it will bring great joy because what you are doing is so special. Attaining enlightenment for the benefit of others is the best activity you can do in this life. All sentient beings will join you in rejoicing because you are dedicating your activities for their benefit. Even though there are already many great bodhisattvas working to benefit all beings, there are infinite numbers of sentient beings who are suffering.

As you develop pure intentions and greater openness, try to expand this attitude without the ego-centeredness of expecting anything in return. Also, whenever you have joyful experiences, you can totally shift your position, mentally transferring your happiness to others and taking others' suffering onto yourself. This is the bodhichitta practice of exchanging self and others.

Loving-kindness and compassion are very special practices that benefit oneself as well as others. When Buddha Shakyamuni taught the benefits of relative bodhichitta, he said that ultimately it results in enlightenment, and relatively it brings eight special results. The first of these is that your body and mind remain relaxed and joyful. The second result of practicing love and compassion is freedom from illness; disease cannot attack you. The third is protection from external attacks through weapons. The fourth is protection from poison — if somebody gives you poison or if you accidentally take poison, it will not kill you.

The fifth result is that you will be greatly appreciated by everyone, not only human beings but nonhuman beings as well. The sixth is that you will be protected by the buddhas and bodhisattvas — the realized beings who have already developed bodhichitta. The seventh benefit is that you will be reborn in the higher realms. The eighth is that all of your wishes will be spontaneously fulfilled; you will achieve whatever you desire without difficulty.

It is important to know the value and qualities of beneficial thoughts and then to practice them. Love and compassion do not develop by just talking about them; they are attitudes that have to be practiced. Whenever you practice meditation, it is important to begin with the intention to become enlightened for the sake of others and to conclude by dedicating the merit to them. If you do this, as you continue to practice you will accumulate immeasurable merit and make rapid progress toward enlightenment.

OM MANI PADME HUNG, mantra of the Buddha of compassion,
Avalokiteshvara (calligraphy by Khenpo Tsewang Dongyal Rinpoche)

The Power of Compassion

Pure compassion has the power to remove all the karmic obscurations and obstacles to enlightenment. As inner wisdom is uncovered, your understanding of relative and absolute truth increases as you progress toward enlightenment. The Buddha said many times that compassion is the most powerful tool for removing ignorance and increasing wisdom.

This is illustrated in a story about Asanga. He was an important Indian scholar born about five hundred years after Buddha, around the beginning of the Christian Era. When Asanga was a young man, he went to Nalanda University, a famous monastery in ancient India and the first real university in the world. Although Asanga became a great scholar, he still had doubts about some of the teachings. He questioned many learned and accomplished masters, but none of them could remove his doubts. He decided to practice the visualization of Maitreya, the future buddha, thinking that once he could see Maitreya he would obtain answers to his questions. After receiving the empowerment and instructions, he went to a mountain in India and meditated on Maitreya for three years.

He thought that after three years he would have enough power to meet Maitreya and ask his questions, but throughout that time he did not receive any signs. After three years he became tired and discouraged, so he left his retreat. On the way down the mountain he came to a village where people were gathered watching an old man making a needle by rubbing a huge iron stick with a piece of silk. Asanga found it hard to believe that someone could make a needle by rubbing an iron rod with a piece of silk, but the old man assured him that it was possible, showing him three needles he had already made. When Asanga saw this example of great patience, he decided to persevere in his practice and he went back to his retreat for another three years.

During the second three years he had some dreams about Maitreya but he still could not see Maitreya. After the second three years he felt bored and tired, and once again he decided to leave. As he came down the mountain he saw a place where water was dripping on a stone. It was dripping very slowly, one drop an hour, but that drip had made a big hole in the rock. When he saw this, it renewed his courage and he decided to go back into retreat for another three years.

This time he had good dreams and other signs, but he still did not see Maitreya clearly enough to ask his questions. Once again he left. On the way down the mountain he saw a small hole in a rock. Around this hole was a shiny mark made by a bird brushing its wings against the rock. This made him renew his resolve to return to his cave for another three years. But after this three-year period he still could not see Maitreya. After twelve years he had no answers, so he left his retreat and went down the mountain.

Along the way he came upon an old dog outside a village. When it barked angrily at him, he saw that the lower part of its body was wounded and covered with fleas and maggots. When he got closer he could see that the dog was suffering terribly and he felt great compassion for it. He thought about all the stories of the Buddha Shakyamuni dedicating himself to sentient beings, and he decided that it was time to dedicate his body to this dog and these insects.

He went to the village and bought a knife. With the knife he cut the flesh on his thigh, thinking that he would remove the worms from the dog and put them on his flesh. Then he realized that if he removed the insects with his fingers, they would die because they were so tender. So he decided to remove them with his tongue. He did not want to look at what he was doing, so he closed his eyes and reached out his tongue toward the dog. But his tongue landed on the ground. He tried again and again, but his tongue kept hitting the ground. Finally, he opened his eyes and the old dog was gone and Buddha Maitreya was there instead.

When he saw Maitreya he was overjoyed, but at the same time he was rather upset. After practicing for so many years, it was only when Asanga saw the old dog that Maitreya had revealed himself. Asanga started crying and asked Maitreya why he had not shown himself sooner. Maitreya replied, "I was not uncompassionate to you. From the first day you arrived at the cave I was always with you. But until today your obscurations blocked your view. Now you see me because of your great compassion for the dog. That compassion removed your obscurations to the point that you can see me." After that, Maitreya personally taught Asanga the texts known as the Five Teachings of Maitreya, which are very important texts in the Tibetan tradition.

Asanga's contact with Maitreya was born of compassion. It was only by compassion that his obscurations were dissolved. For this reason Guru Padmasambhava taught that without compassion, dharma practice will not bear fruit, and in fact, without compassion your practice will become rotten.

Tara, female symbol of compassionate activity

The Inseparability of Compassion and Emptiness

Compassion is the beneficial thought that moves you to help other sentient beings. It arises when you see their misery and pain, and you feel from the depth of your heart that you want to remove that suffering.

Compassion can be divided into three types. The first is compassion that focuses on sentient beings, the second is compassion that focuses on ignorance, and the third is compassion without any focus. The first type of compassion is easy to understand; if we look closely at the painful situations that sentient beings experience, we feel compassion and want to change their miserable conditions.

The second kind of compassion is directed toward a deeper level; it is compassion for the ignorance that sentient beings have about the true nature of phenomena. Everything about their bodies, possessions, and emotions is constantly changing, but due to ignorance, sentient beings grasp and cling to their lives as if they will last for aeons. Then, when things change, they suffer. This type of compassion focuses on ignorance as the root of all suffering.

The third type of compassion is objectless compassion. The first two types of compassion have objects: the first has the suffering of sentient beings and the second has their ignorance, but the third type has no particular focus. It is the deepest level of compassion; it is the meditation on the absolute state of equanimity. With this kind of compassion there are no distinctions between sentient beings and nonsentient beings; one's compassion is equal for all. One simply rests in the absolute, natural state, without any particular ideas or judgments. This compassion arises from the realization of emptiness and is free from all desire and duality. This level of meditation is achieved gradually and it is not as easy to understand as the first two types of compassion.

Practicing compassion will bring about the recognition of emptiness as the true nature of the mind. When you practice virtuous actions of love and compassion on the relative level, you spontaneously realize the profound nature of emptiness, which is the absolute level. In turn, if you focus your meditation practice on emptiness, then your loving-kindness and compassion will spontaneously grow.

These two natures, the absolute and the relative, are not opposites; they always arise together. They have the same nature; they are inseparable like a fire and its heat or the sun and its light. Compassion and emptiness are not like two sides of a coin. Emptiness and compassion are not two separate elements joined together; they are always coexistent.

In Buddhism, emptiness does not mean the absence of apparent existence. Emptiness is not like a black hole or darkness, or like an empty house or an empty bottle. Emptiness is fullness and openness and flexibility. Because of emptiness it is possible for phenomena to function, for beings to see and hear, and for things to move and change. It is called emptiness because when we examine things we cannot find anything that substantially and solidly exists. There is nothing that has a truly existent nature. Everything we perceive appears through ever-changing causes and conditions, without an independent, solid basis. Although from a relative perspective things appear, they arise from emptiness and they dissolve into emptiness. All appearances are like water bubbles or the reflection of the moon in water.

Buddhist logic analyzes objects, both physical and mental, to see whether a truly existent essence can be found. One can mentally break down a physical object until it is only atoms, and those atoms can be divided into subtle atoms, and those can be analyzed until there is nothing at all. Objects are designated as such only by the imagination. External objects do not exist the way we believe them to be — as solid, singular, and permanent. If we look deeper, whatever appears is not truly there; it is a sort of hallucination.

Once we understand the emptiness of outer forms, we should look at the mind itself. What is the mind? Where is it? In analyzing its various aspects, we cannot find the mind of the past or the future, or even the mind of the present moment. The mind is also empty of substantial existence; it cannot be grasped. Everything, including the mind, is ultimately illusory and imaginary.

This understanding of relative and absolute truth can be applied in practical ways. For example, when you find yourself getting angry at someone, if you look immediately at the nature of your mind, you will not be able to find any substantial anger or anyone who is getting angry. If you really see that anger is empty by nature, then the anger will dissolve itself. The best way to eliminate negative emotions is by recognizing their emptiness. This is approaching disturbing emotions on the absolute level. To approach them on the relative level by using compassion as an antidote can also be very helpful. After the emotional energy has subsided somewhat, you could think compassionately: "I shouldn't feel angry because this person is acting out of ignorance. Because she doesn't see clearly, she doesn't know what is appropriate, and this conflict has arisen. I wish she could be free from all ignorance and suffering."

Buddha Shakyamuni explained the union of appearance and emptiness in the *Heart Sutra*. This text begins with the Buddha entering the samadhi of profound illumination, and by the power of that samadhi Shariputra had the wisdom to ask Avalokiteshvara how a bodhisattva should train in perfect wisdom. Even though Avalokiteshvara gave the explanation, since it was due to the power of the Buddha's meditation that Shariputra asked the question, this sutra is considered to be the Buddha's teaching.

In the *Heart Sutra* Avalokiteshvara explained that form is emptiness and emptiness is form; emptiness is not different than form, and form is not different than emptiness. Whatever we see is empty of inherent nature and yet it clearly appears. There is nothing solid to hold onto, yet things continue to manifest. If this is true, why do we cling to people and things as being real? It is because of a wrong understanding. This mistaken view is what we need to break down, so that we see whatever appears in an open and impartial way. It is extremely important to realize emptiness as the true nature of reality.

The great meditation master and scholar Nagarjuna said that phenomena are actually nothing, that on the absolute level they are emptiness, yet on the relative level they appear and function. Since all appearances are empty by nature, the relative and absolute aspects are inseparably united. One could never find emptiness without appearance or appearance without emptiness.

In terms of practice, the wish to attain enlightenment for the sake of others and the cultivation of love and compassion are the relative practice, and meditation on great emptiness is the absolute practice. When you maintain the natural state of mind in meditation, then compassion and loving-kindness spontaneously radiate. When you practice immeasurable love and compassion for others, then the emptiness nature of all phenomena becomes clear. As much as possible you should practice with the understanding that compassion and emptiness are inseparable.

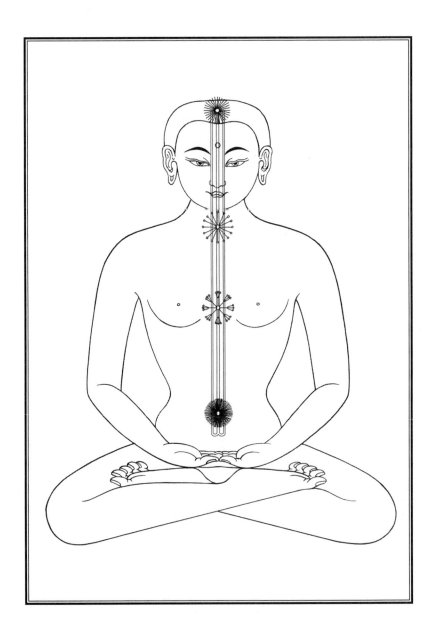

Three main channels and four chakras

The Channels and Winds

According to the tantric Buddhist system, of all the aspects of the body — its bones, muscles, blood, and so on, the three principal aspects are the channels, the wind, and the essence element. The channels are the most important because they carry the wind, which moves the essence element throughout the body. When the channels are perfectly balanced, then the wind energy and the essence element are also balanced.

The channels, or the nervous system, are like the roots of the body. There are 1,072 major channels in the body. When a baby is conceived from the initial mingling of consciousness with the two elements of the parents in the mother's womb, the first things that form are the channels. The first channel that appears in the fetus is the navel channel. Right after that, the two channels of the eyes are formed. These three main channels, the navel channel and the two channels of the eyes, are the foundation of the body. As a baby grows, each week there are major developments and changes inside the mother's womb, and gradually the other large channels form until the body structure is complete.

According to the inner teachings of the vajrayana, the body has three main channels. The most important is the central channel, which is known as the *avadhuti* in Sanskrit and as the *uma* in Tibetan. The central channel starts four fingers below the navel and goes straight up to the top of the head. On the right side of the central channel there is another channel, in which the white elements of the body flow. It is half as big around as the central channel, and it goes up to the head and comes down to the right nostril. The third major channel is on the left side of the central channel. It is the same size as the right channel, and it goes up to the head and down to the left nostril. The left channel is red, since the red elements of the body pass through it.

The four chakras, or wheels of the channels, are joined to the three channels. At the crown of the head is the "crown chakra of great bliss," which has thirty-two spokes or petals. The second chakra is the "enjoyment chakra," which is located in the throat and has sixteen spokes. The third chakra is called the "dharma chakra," and it is in the heart center. This chakra has eight spokes, which are related to the heart as well as to the main channels. The fourth chakra is the navel chakra, with sixty-four spokes or petals. It is called the "manifestation chakra" because it is the source of everything you experience; everything is reflected or manifested from that center.

The three channels and four chakras are the basic ground of the body; they are the source and the main condition for all of one's experiences and sense consciousnesses. In all human beings, the three major channels and the four chakras are basically structured in the same way. However, the minor channels are formed differently in different people. Because of differences in the minor channels, people have different personalities, different ways of talking and acting, and different experiences.

All human beings generally see the same things. When people look at a tree or a flower, they see a similar object because the three channels and four chakras are similar. However, since the minor channels function differently in the way they join the main channels and chakras, some people find an object interesting or beautiful while others do not. People have different tastes, experiences, and understandings based on the different formations of the small channels in their bodies.

This applies only to human beings. If we look at the way animals perceive, they see objects differently than humans because their channels are structured differently. For example, humans can see the five basic colors, but animals do not see them. Buddha Shakyamuni taught that the beings in each of the six realms see a predominantly different color. For example, hell beings see mostly black colors. The hungry ghosts see mostly a dark red color. The animals see mostly a dark green color. Only in the higher realms of the humans, jealous gods, and gods do beings see all five colors. And in the god realm, the gods see more white color along with the other colors.

The reason the various classes of beings in the six realms see different colors is because color and vision are dependent upon the structure of the channels. Things like colors do not actually exist externally. On the absolute level, in reality, your vision of things like colors comes from inside. Your vision reflects out and you see things externally. This is one reason why the channels are important. If you know about the channels and can control them, then you will have more control of your vision and your experience, and you will not be as confused. Keeping an erect body posture is an important factor in balancing the channels and chakras.

When your channels are perfectly balanced, the wind energy becomes more gentle and normal. The breath or wind energy is an important element of the body because it communicates between the outside and the inside of the body. Your whole body, as well as your consciousness, relies upon the breath. The wind energy and the mind travel together through the channels.

In the vajrayana teachings there is a well-known example for the relationship between the body, the channels, the wind, and the mind. The body is like the ground or the earth, the channels are like the roads, the wind is like a horse, and the mind or consciousness is like a person who is riding the horse. If the horse is wild, the person is carried in all directions, wherever the horse ends up going. Similarly, if the wind is unbalanced, the consciousness is carried by the wind through all the channels of the body. But if the wind element is tamed, then the mind that rides on the wind is tame as well.

The goal of meditation practice is to bring everything into the natural state. In order to do this it is important to know how the channels dominate the body, and second, how the wind energy affects the mind. One way in which the wind element affects the mind is that it establishes your sense of time. The wind element manifests as the pulse, and each beat of the pulse is considered to be one second. The watch that you wear is like a duplicate of your pulse. Time is reflected externally so that you experience minutes, hours, months, and years, but actually, your sense of time depends upon your inner state.

It is said that a healthy adult breathes twelve times a minute, counting the inhalation and exhalation as one breath. Adding it up, we find that people breathe many thousands of times every day. Most of the winds are connected with the emotions, but about every two hundred breaths there is a breath of wisdom wind. If you know about the wind energy, you can calculate the wisdom wind perfectly. By recognizing the wisdom wind, you can linger in that moment or use that wisdom wind to transform the rest of your emotional winds into the wisdom wind.

There are many vajrayana techniques connected with the wind energy, such as the *bum chen*, the big vase practice, and the *bum chung*, the small vase practice. These bring extraordinary physical powers. For example, experts on the wind energy can travel long distances very quickly. If it normally takes one week to walk somewhere, they can walk that far in one day. Through controlling their winds, they can levitate and fly in the sky, and their bodies become younger and more healthy, with less wrinkles and gray hair.

The dzogchen tradition teaches the importance of four levels of straightness: when the body becomes straight, then the channels become straight. When the channels become straight, then the wind energy becomes straight. When the wind element becomes straight, then the mind becomes straight and primordial wisdom shines out.

However, samsara is not really straight; it is always circling back on itself. In the vajrayana tradition there is an illustration called the "wheel of life," which depicts samsara. In the center of the wheel of life there are three animals — a pig, a rooster, and a snake, which are coming out of each others' mouths and circling around. These animals represent the three poisons. The pig is a symbol of ignorance, the source of samsara. Ignorance gives birth to attachment, which is symbolized by the rooster. Anger develops from attachment, in that whatever prevents the fulfillment of desire becomes an object of anger. Anger is symbolized by the snake. The interconnection of these three shows ignorance as the root of samsaric existence, giving rise again and again to confused emotions and actions.

To step out of the circle of samsara, we need to straighten and balance the body, the channels, and the wind. At the same time we must train in compassion and loving-kindness for all beings. If we balance the wind energy and the channels, and practice loving-kindness and compassion, then enlightenment will certainly follow.

Vimalamitra, early dzogchen master

Meditation Posture
and Breath Purification

When meditating, it is always important to keep your body, speech, and mind balanced. The body has three principal components: the channels, the wind, and the essence element. If these three components are well-balanced, you will feel healthy and comfortable.

First, the channels need to be properly aligned by maintaining good posture. The main points of good posture are known as the seven-point posture of Buddha Vairochana. If you use these postures when you meditate, your meditation will be stable and smooth.

The first point is to sit with your legs crossed in the lotus, or vajra, posture. Second, your back should be kept very straight, not bent forward or back, but straight like an arrow pointing up to the sky. Third is the hand position, or mudra. There are two popular ways to hold the hands. The equanimity mudra is done by placing the right hand on top of the left hand, with the palms up and both hands resting in your lap, close to the navel. Or you can rest your hands on your knees with the palms down, in what is called the relaxing mudra.

Fourth, you should keep your elbows rounded, not touching them to your sides. The angle of your elbows is sometimes compared to the way a vulture holds its wings when landing. Fifth, your neck should be held straight, keeping the crown chakra straight up. To keep your head aligned properly you can bend your head forward a little so that your chest is a bit down. Sixth, keep your eyes looking forward and down toward the tip of your nose, without blinking a lot or moving your eyes in different directions. And last, hold your tongue so that it touches the upper roof of your mouth. The lips may be slightly parted.

Once you know how to balance the channels with good posture, the next aspect to balance is the breath. While you are meditating, continue to breathe normally, without changing the way you usually breathe. When you begin your morning practice session, after doing at least three prostrations and sitting on your cushion with correct posture, it is good to do a breath purification exercise. There is a particular dzogchen technique for breath purification that releases the inner air of the negative emotions. The three main emotions, often called the three poisons, are attachment, anger, and ignorance. By releasing the air connected with the three poisons you can clarify your wind energy.

To begin this exercise, form your hands into the gesture, or mudra, called "the vajra fist." The word *vajra* means "indestructible," so the vajra fist is a gesture of indestructibility. Press your thumb at the base of your ring finger and curl your hand into a first. The ring finger is especially important because it has particular channels related to the emotions. When you press your thumb on your ring finger, you are blocking the emotion channels.

Having formed the vajra fist with both hands, place your hands, with the fingers facing up, at your hips. The hips also have many channels, including emotion channels; pressing the vajra fist on the hips blocks these emotion channels and helps the mind to relax further. After pressing down on your hips, rub the back side of your fists along your thighs to your knees. Then turn your fists over, bring your fists back along your thighs, and gradually pull your fists up your body until they reach the chest level, and then thrust your hands out in front of you and extend your fingers. You should extend your arms and fingers very straight, shooting them out like arrows.

Then, drop both hands to your knees. Leaving your right hand on your right knee, raise your left hand and rotate it in the lotus-turning mudra, and then press the thumb over the base of the ring finger and extend the index finger. Press your left nostril with your left index finger, and release air through your right nostril.

The channel located on the right of the central channel is filled with the body's white element and the wind connected with anger, so you release the anger air through the right nostril. While exhaling, visualize that all the anger air passing out of the right nostril is colored dark yellow, the color that represents anger. All of it goes out, so that no anger wind is left inside.

After that, you press down again at your hips with both hands in the vajra fist and repeat the sequence of drawing your fists to your knees, back up to your chest, shooting out your arms, and dropping your hands to your knees. But this time leave your left hand on your left knee and do the lotus-turning mudra with your right hand. Place your right thumb over the base of your right ring finger, press your right index finger to your right nostril, and exhale through the left nostril. The left side of the body is dominated by attachment and desire. The left channel is red in color, being filled with the red element of the body. By exhaling through the left nostril you release the attachment air which is visualized as dark red in color.

Then, do the same sequence of pressing down and bringing both arms up and shooting them out. The third time you leave both hands on your knees and release air from both nostrils as well as from your mouth. This time the air of ignorance is expelled. The energy of ignorance is not located particularly on the right or the left side because ignorance pervades everywhere. Since ignorance is the ground of both attachment and anger, it is released from both nostrils as well as the mouth. The ignorance air is visualized as dark blue in color.

Doing this exercise will help to clear the air of the emotions. When the emotion air is dispelled, at that moment wisdom air will appear more clearly. After doing this exercise to purify the breath, your mind will be clearer and calmer, and it will be easier to maintain your mind in the meditative state. Even though this purification exercise is very simple, it is very beneficial.

After doing the breath purification, you are ready to begin your practice. Just as you clean and decorate your house before a guest arrives, similarly, before beginning to meditate you should make the proper preparations for the principal guest, your inner wisdom. The many channels in your body are filled with different emotions and airs, so it is important to purify the stale air and bring fresh wisdom air into the body.

The Tibetan "Ah" syllable, the first letter of the Tibetan alphabet
(calligraphy by Khenchen Palden Sherab Rinpoche)

Meditating on the
True Nature of the Mind

Once the body, channels, and wind are balanced, the next step is to keep your mind in the natural state through meditation. By simply maintaining the mind as it is, without adding or subtracting anything, one will reach the inner nature, which is unchanging and indestructible.

The instructions for this type of meditation are very simple. One begins by sitting with good posture on a cushion, because it is important to stay straight. Then, one simply maintains the natural clarity of the mind, without analyzing one's experiences or being disturbed by thoughts. In the dzogchen style of meditation, there is actually nothing to do except relax in the mind's nature of clarity and emptiness. Inner awareness is different than external awareness; it is called clear-light emptiness. It is helpful to use the sky as an analogy for the true nature of the mind — when you let your mind mingle with the open space of the sky, you do not need any particular focus. Simply maintain the mind naturally, without discrimination or judgments, and experience its nature as being spacious as the sky.

Meditating on the nature of the mind is something you can do anytime. You do not have to go somewhere special to acquire the nature of the mind; you do not need to buy it from a store or dig it up from the earth; it is always available. During meditation you do not need to think any particular thoughts or make any effort to change what you are. Just simply maintain where you are and what you are, without trying to do anything unusual. If you meditate by simply maintaining the natural state, then everything unnatural will be removed. You do not have to do anything except remain on your cushion. In one sense this is something of a joke, but in another sense it is true. You simply relax on your cushion, and that's it!

Although meditation does not demand any physical activity, you do have to maintain the meditative state, and this takes some effort. Effort is not actually part of the basic ground nature, but since our obscurations and ignorance are so strong it requires effort to make meditation natural. When meditating in this way, it is not necessary to fight with the obscurations. As your practice develops power, it will spontaneously remove the obscurations since they are not part of the primordial nature. This practice will reveal more and more of the basic ground of primordial wisdom. The rising sun does not fight with the darkness; just as its presence makes darkness disappear, in the same way, when we meditate, the presence of the primordial nature overcomes ignorance. It is like the heat of the sun in springtime penetrating the cold ground so that green plants naturally begin to grow. When meditation practice causes primordial wisdom to shine, the enlightened qualities manifest according to one's level of meditative stabilization.

The natural mind is inexpressible and inconceivable. It cannot be expressed verbally, but it can be experienced through your own awareness. When you meditate you should not follow your monkeylike thoughts; instead try to remain in a state of mindful awareness all the time. Of course, at some point you will begin thinking, but try not to analyze or follow your thoughts; simply watch with the mind. This is called mindfulness. Mindfulness means that the mind is watching how the meditation is going.

Do your meditation with a relaxed mind; do not worry or force yourself to meditate. Do not be in a rush, but be concerned enough that you do not postpone it until tomorrow. If you put it off, there is always another tomorrow, and you can extend that for endless tomorrows without developing your practice. Once in a while it is good to watch your meditation and see how it is going, but do not do this all the time because that is spying too much. On the other hand, you should not be so relaxed that you are careless, since that will not bring good results either. There has to be a balance.

There is a story that illustrates this from the lifetime of the Buddha. There was a monk who thought he should meditate forcefully, and his mind got twisted and tight. He did not feel he was progressing in his practice, so he told one of his fellow monks about his concerns. His friend advised him not to meditate so tightly, but to be more relaxed. Then the monk meditated in a very relaxed way, but he still did not get good results. Since he was very interested in meditation he got upset about his lack of progress, and finally he went to the Buddha and explained his trouble. The Buddha asked him, "Before you were a monk, what was your expertise?" The monk replied, "I was an expert on the mandolin." The Buddha asked him, "When the mandolin is strung very tight, will it make a beautiful sound?" And the monk answered, "Not if you use too much tension." Then the Buddha asked, "If the strings are loose, will it make a good sound?" The monk replied, "No, of course not. You have to keep the proper tension on the strings." The Buddha told him, "Meditation is the same way: you have to keep the proper balance — not too tight and not too loose."

When you meditate with the proper balance you can reach enlightenment and discover the primordial nature. As a beginner, it is best to practice for many short periods and gradually extend the sessions to longer and longer periods of time. Meditate for as long as you have time, and when you finish, dedicate the merit for the benefit of all sentient beings. Buddhist meditation is always based on love for all beings, so you should conclude your practice with thoughts of compassion and loving-kindness. When you dedicate the merit to others, it does not mean that you lose that merit, actually it multiplies your merit. So it is good to always complete your meditation session by spending a few minutes dedicating the merit for the benefit of all sentient beings.

"Joyful effort" (calligraphy by Khenpo Tsewang Dongyal Rinpoche)

The Five Supports
of Meditation

All beings have the potential for buddhahood. In order to actualize this potential we need to meditate. The best supports for meditation practice are joyful effort, mindfulness, devotion, concentration, and wisdom. The Buddha taught that we can actualize enlightenment with these five supports.

When you meditate, first you need to apply joyful and continuous effort. In any activity you need a certain amount of motivation to finish what you start. If you experience joy in what you are doing, then you will want to continue. Joyful effort is not accomplished by rushing around and staying busy; the best type of effort is steady and smooth, like a river. When you look at a wide river, its movement is very subtle; even though you may not be able to tell whether it is moving or not, its movement is very powerful. When you develop joyful interest and ongoing effort, your practice will bring good results.

It is also important not to expect immediate results. Practicing strenuously for a short time and then dropping it altogether will not bring lasting results. It is like a fire made with hay — it blazes up very fast, but the heat does not last. When you first begin to practice, you should meditate frequently for short periods of time. Do not start with a huge amount of time and then decrease it; start with a small amount of time and gradually increase it. Guru Padmasambhava taught this shortly before he departed from Tibet. The Queen of Tibet, Ngang-zang Palgyi Gyalmo, asked Guru Padmasambhava to tell her how to meditate. He told her to begin by meditating often for very short periods. He used the example of a leaky roof in an old house, where the rain does not pour in, but leaks in drop by drop. This is how you should begin to meditate, and then gradually extend the time.

No matter how long you meditate, try to meditate with mindfulness. Otherwise, if you are just sitting on your cushion and thinking, then your mind will travel all over. This is called the monkey mind. People say that monkeys are always active; they never really rest, even when they sit still. For whatever amount of time you meditate, even for five or ten minutes, try to maintain your mind single-pointedly, without being distracted by thoughts.

Of course, it naturally happens when you meditate that thoughts suddenly arise and lead you in different directions. When you see that happening, rather than following the thoughts, immediately bring the mind back through mindfulness. The reason you need to meditate is because concepts have covered up the natural state. If thoughts did not cause confusion, you would not need to meditate. However, you should not be upset or sad when thoughts arise. It is quite normal for thoughts to arise during meditation. The main point is to not follow the thoughts.

It is also important in meditation to have the right motivation, which is based on devotion and bodhichitta. Devotion to the highly realized beings such as Buddha Shakyamuni, Guru Padmasambhava, or Tara means that you feel close to them and wish to attain the same ability they have to help all sentient beings. Devotion is feeling great interest in their realization and longing to have the same realization as soon as you can.

Devotion combines interest and clarity of mind. It develops in two ways. Some people develop devotion with the assistance of spiritual friends who encourage them to study the teachings and follow the examples of the great masters in order to reach enlightenment. In other cases, devotion develops spontaneously in an individual.

In addition to devotion to the Buddha, dharma, and sangha, in the vajrayana there is also devotion to what is called the three roots — the lama, the deities, and the dakinis. The three roots are the three principal objects of refuge in Buddhist tantra. Devotion is like a channel that brings down the blessings of realized beings. Even at the level of dzogchen, devotion is very important. Devotion is like the key which opens the door of enlightenment. In the *Prajñaparamita Sutra,* Buddha Shakyamuni taught that devotion is like a light that makes enlightenment visible.

Devotion is important because if you have devotion, then you can receive blessings. There is a story that long ago in Tibet a student approached a famous Kadampa master and asked, "Great master, could you give me some blessings?" And the master replied, "Well, noble student, could you give me some devotion?" Another example of devotion that you may know is the life story of Milarepa. His teacher Marpa did many things to test his confidence and devotion, but Milarepa's devotion was very strong, and as a result he achieved great realization.

Joyful effort is a natural extension of devotion. As your interest and sense of purpose grow, you feel good about working harder. A person who thinks clearly about the dharma and desires to understand it will take concrete steps to know the dharma at deeper and deeper levels. With joyful effort, you can overcome physical and mental obstacles quite happily in order to accomplish your spiritual goal.

Even if people have devotion and joyful effort, without proper mindfulness they will not be able to accomplish their objective. Mindfulness means paying attention to the main focus of the meditation as well as to the supports of devotion, effort, concentration, and so forth. Mindfulness means not forgetting what you are doing, but being clear and focused. It fulfills devotion and joyful effort by giving the practice a sharper focus and direction.

Concentration means continually maintaining an unmoving focus. To accomplish concentration in meditation you need devotion, joyful effort, and mindfulness; without these, concentration is impossible. For example, devotion is the initial interest people feel toward spiritual practice. Joyful effort naturally follows when they plan to meditate, set a schedule, and actually sit down and practice. But not all sitting is good meditation; sometimes people fall asleep or their minds wander. Good meditation needs mindfulness to keep the attention focused and on track. When devotion, joyful effort, and mindfulness are practiced, then concentration is present and the mind is smooth and stable. Generally, our minds are darting about and unstable. Concentration naturally brings calmness and peace of mind.

The fifth power, wisdom, naturally emerges from practicing the first four powers. One way to understand wisdom is to divide it into its two aspects, relative and absolute. Together these make up true wisdom, but it is important to understand the characteristics of each aspect through direct perception and inference.

Relatively, we directly perceive objects through seeing, hearing, smelling, tasting, and touching. We apply inference when we think about them. These are aspects of relative wisdom. When we examine phenomena closely, we see that they exist in an illusory way, like a mirage, a dream, or the reflection of the moon in water. Recognition of the illusory nature of phenomena is absolute wisdom. We can use logical inference to understand the relative nature of phenomena, but reasoning cannot encompass the absolute nature. Inference about emptiness can lead closer to the absolute truth, but direct perception is necessary to realize it since the true nature transcends dualistic thinking. Wisdom is understanding the absolute and relative truths, and recognizing their differences as well as how they are united.

To get a better understanding of the five powers, it is helpful to look at their opposites. The opposite of devotion is the absence of interest and clear thinking about spiritual practice. People who lack devotion see only the ordinary objects right in front of them; their vision of the deeper levels of reality is obscured. Buddha Shakyamuni taught that devotion opens the door to pure vision. The future buddha, the bodhisattva

Maitreya, said that people without devotion are like a burned seed. Just as a burned seed cannot grow or produce any fruit, in the same way a person without devotion cannot progress on the spiritual path.

The opposite of joyful effort is laziness, or feeling dull and heavy. There are different forms of laziness. One form is when you have an interest in practicing, but feel you do not have the time now and will do it later. This is just postponing your accomplishment. Another form of laziness is being hard on yourself and ignoring your good qualities, thinking that you are not good enough to practice. A third type of laziness is just following old habits and refusing to make the effort to change, like preferring to be comfortable by staying in bed. Refusing to think new thoughts or act differently is also laziness.

The opposite of mindfulness is forgetfulness. Forgetfulness happens because the mind is moving so fast. The mind is somewhat like a strainer that cannot keep water from flowing out. As soon as one thought passes away another takes its place. As a result we do not spend enough time thinking clearly about what is important, so we neglect the things we really want to do. We need to firmly imprint on our mind what is truly important. For example, after hearing a dharma talk or meditation instruction we should spend some time reviewing the meaning of what we heard. Then we will not forget it so quickly.

The opposite of concentration is distraction. Buddha Shakyamuni mentioned many types of distractions, but the two most common are external and internal distractions. The external distractions are objects of the five senses, which bring up feelings of attraction and revulsion. Internal distractions are objects of our imagination, which bring up attachment and anger, hope and fear. Everyone has distracting thoughts; they are not unusual. Having thoughts while meditating is not a problem, but nurturing them and indulging in them is a problem. We must make a firm decision and exert strong effort to overcome distractions during practice. Good concentration eliminates the emotions so that one is not distracted by one's feelings. Then, the mind can remain perfectly balanced and focused in one direction.

The opposite of wisdom is ignorance. Ignorance is the root of samsara — the process of endless birth and death and rebirth. Ignorance is like the darkness caused by wearing a hat that completely covers our head so that we cannot see anything. Or it is like being in a room with no openings. However, ignorance is not something solid, but an illusion that can disappear when it is penetrated with awareness. When ignorance is removed, then wisdom shines forth and the emptiness nature is apparent.

Since emptiness is free from all duality, it is the supreme state of equanimity where there is no discrimination or conflict. It is a state of complete openness in which everything is radiating and reflecting. In the *Heart Sutra,* Buddha Shakyamuni taught, "Form is emptiness; emptiness is form." The forms we perceive with our senses are inseparable from emptiness; this is the essence of the primordial nature.

Each of us has a strong inclination to feel separate. By holding on to the feeling of having an ego we also create the egos of others and develop dualistic thinking. We distinguish in various ways between self and others, between my interests and the interests of others, and we divide others into friends and enemies. This is how we develop a dualistic world. But from the point of view of emptiness, there is no real basis for dualistic thinking; there is no truly existing self in oneself or others. The idea of a separate self is a temporary creation of our deluded minds, and this ignorant thought produces grasping and attachment. Ignorance means not knowing emptiness, which is the true nature of things. When ignorance, the root of all human problems, is removed by the wisdom of emptiness, then one experiences great equanimity.

Chetsun Senge Wangchuk, early dzogchen master

Shamatha and Vipashyana

Buddha Shakyamuni expounded many different levels of instruction in order to teach us how to maintain the true nature of mind and show compassion for all sentient beings. There are many different meditations for this purpose, such as shamatha and vipashyana, and the creation stage and the completion stage practices of the vajrayana. All these methods have only one object, which is to reveal the true nature of the mind. These different techniques are related to each other and they work together to help attain enlightenment.

When first learning to meditate, most people find it difficult to rest the mind so that the primordial wisdom can shine through. Thoughts continuously arise, one after another, like waves on the ocean, and the mind is constantly moving. It helps to begin by sitting with good posture and then to remain focused. There are several techniques in the Buddhist tradition for settling the mind and uncovering wisdom. Two of the best known are shamatha and vipashyana.

Understanding the meaning of the Sanskrit terms can help us to understand the way in which we need to meditate. The Sanskrit word *shamatha* is made of two words, *shama* and *tha*. *Shama* means "peaceful or calm," and *tha* means "letting or abiding," so *shamatha* means "letting the mind be peaceful." Shamatha is also known in Sanskrit as *samadhi*, which is also two words put together. *Sama* means "motionless" and *dhi* means "holding," so *samadhi* refers to maintaining one's mind in a constant, unchanging state. For example, if you fill a bowl with water and do not touch it, the water does not move, it stays still. Similarly, when your mind rests single-pointedly, undisturbed by thoughts, it becomes calm.

In this state the mind is concentrated and focused. This means that the mind does not move or change; it is solid like a mountain.

Maintaining the mind in a state of stillness results in the clarity of the natural mind shining forth. However, most of us do not experience stillness; our minds are as active as a hurricane. When the mind is very active, we cannot maintain calmness and, in fact, many of our activities cause sorrow and strife. Sometimes we get discouraged when we experience difficulty in maintaining calmness. Although it is difficult, all of us have the ability to calm the mind; it can be done with joyful effort and courage. Achieving anything in dharma practice or in the world requires effort and perseverance. It is important to believe that we can accomplish this goal and then to exert effort and continue to the end.

In the *Prajnaparamita Sutra* the Buddha gave an example of courageous effort. There was a bodhisattva who taught that if one could remove a mountain then one could attain enlightenment. Some people thought this was impossible, so they gave up and did not reach enlightenment. Other people heard the same thing, and with great effort, patience and courage, removed the mountain and attained enlightenment. Although calming the mind may seem as difficult to us as removing a mountain, if we have patience and courage and joyful effort, we will be able to achieve our goal.

There are many stages in mental development, but as soon as we are able to maintain the mind in a calm state, at that very moment there is joy and peace. This is reflected in the body becoming relaxed, and then the mind becomes more relaxed. Since the mind and body influence each other, as the mind calms down, the hidden enlightened qualities emerge more and more.

To do the shamatha technique you begin with good sitting posture. Use the seven-point posture of Buddha Vairochana, with the back straight, the hands on the knees, and so on, and continue to breathe normally. There are two ways to do shamatha practice: with an object of focus and without an object of focus. Shamatha with an object involves concentrating on a physical object like a small piece of crystal, a statue of the Buddha, or a picture of Guru Padmasambhava, or you can concentrate on a visualized object like a small circle of light or a small syllable made of light. Another technique for doing shamatha with an object is to follow the breath, consciously recognizing your inhalations and exhalations. No matter which sort of object you use, whenever your mind wanders you bring it back to the object of concentration and maintain it there for as long as you can. Shamatha without an object has no particular focus; it is just meditating on emptiness.

The second type of meditation is called vipashyana. *Vipashyana* is a Sanskrit word made up of *vi*, meaning "extraordinary," and *pashyana*, meaning "seeing." Literally, it means "extraordinary seeing," but it is usually translated into English as "insight" or "supreme seeing." Vipashyana goes further than maintaining a calm and unmoving mind. In vipashyana practice you examine the mind and its source. By penetrating the surface level of thoughts and emotions, you see that their insubstantiality is the true nature of the mind. This is the practice of extraordinary seeing, in which you realize that everything arises from great emptiness, and that the true nature of the mind is unborn, unceasing, and free from concepts. When the mind relaxes in its natural state, all of the usual perceptions of solid existence are experienced as nothing more than a dream. This is the great equanimity free from mental fabrications.

The technique for vipashyana begins the same as with shamatha, with good sitting posture and normal breathing, and then you look into the mind itself. When thoughts and emotions appear, you look for their origin and their destination. Where do they come from and where do they go? When you look into the mind in this way, you reach the true nature of the mind. Then, simply relax effortlessly in this state, having confidence in the true nature, knowing that there is actually nothing to gain and nothing to lose. This is the original state from which we all come, the state where the whole universe originates. If you meditate in this way without effort or fear or discomfort, you will discover that everything exists in one state of equanimity that transcends suffering.

Vipashyana meditation transcends ordinary thinking by seeing the illusory nature of all mental fabrications. It sees beyond the distinctions we make between self and others, enemies and friends, good and bad, and so on. For example, although mountains and trees appear as solidly existing, substantial objects, in reality their existence is more like a reflection of the moon in water. All physical objects can be divided into smaller and smaller parts until they cannot be found anymore. What we called a mountain is just a mental designation that does not exist separately from the mind. Just as there is no independently existing mountain, there is also no independently existing mind. Our mind is insubstantial and cannot be grasped, just like a reflection in water. The phenomenal world and the mind are both based on emptiness. All distinctions between subject and object are ultimately empty of true existence. When we know this clearly through meditation, we are practicing vipashyana.

Shamatha and vipashyana are closely connected. By shamatha one maintains the mind in the natural state, and by vipashyana one sees that all appearances are insubstantial emptiness. Success with one of these practices supports the development of the other, but the result of vipashyana meditation is greater than that of shamatha. The realization resulting from vipashyana is sometimes called "the third eye," which means that one has visions and experiences that transcend one's previous, ordinary perceptions.

Shamatha and vipashyana are taught in both the sutrayana and vajrayana teachings, although they are more related to the sutrayana. The sutrayana is another name for the hinayana and mahayana teachings of the Buddha. All of the sutrayana is included in the vajrayana, which is considered the highest of the yanas.

Vajrasattva

Ngondro Practice

The ngondro practices are the preliminary practices of the vajrayana. The usual approach in Tibet is to start formal practice with ngondro, and while doing ngondro you also do shamatha and vipashyana as part of ngondro. In all vajrayana practices, after the main part of the practice, there is a concluding section of shamatha and vipashyana. These are done according to the type of meditation you are doing, the instructions of your teacher, and your level of accomplishment.

Previous great masters like Guru Padmasambhava extracted the essential teachings of the sutras and tantras and condensed them into the ngondro. *Ngondro* is a compound word in Tibetan, made up of *ngon*, which means "before," and *dro*, which means "to go." Together they mean "that which goes before" or "preliminary." Looking at the meaning in a larger way, the ngondro practices "go before" because they must be done before reaching enlightenment. If these practices go first, then enlightenment will follow. Many people translate *ngondro* as "preliminary" because these are the first set of vajrayana practices. Ngondro is used to establish a firm foundation for further realization.

Ngondro practice has several parts. The first part is called the four methods for reversing one's thoughts from samsara. The next section is taking refuge in the Buddha, dharma, and sangha, and then in the gurus, deities, and dakinis. The third section is developing bodhichitta, a special teaching of the mahayana, which is the beneficial thought of caring more for others than for yourself. The fourth section is the mandala offering, which is particularly connected with accumulating merit and wisdom. The fifth section is the practice of Buddha Vajrasattva, who is a special deity or buddha of the vajrayana tradition. Vajrasattva has the special power of being able to purify obscurations and negative actions. The sixth section is the practice of guru yoga, which is very important for receiving the blessings and realization of the vajrayana teachings.

An important part of ngondro is prostration practice. According to the ancient masters you can do prostrations while reciting the refuge prayers or in the guru yoga section while saying the Vajra Guru Mantra. Prostrations are particularly aimed at removing body obscurations and releasing the knots in the channels.

At the end of every session of ngondro, you should dedicate the merit accumulated by the practice for the benefit of all beings, wishing that their suffering will be removed and that they will attain the perfect happiness of enlightenment. Also, during every session of ngondro practice you meditate on the true nature of the mind. Even if there is not time to do shamatha and vipashyana after each part, formless practice should definitely be done after the Vajrasattva and guru yoga practices.

The stability of shamatha and the higher seeing of vipashyana are also part of the vajrayana visualization practices. When you visualize Guru Padmasambhava and concentrate on his image, that is a form of shamatha meditation. At the end of the session, when you dissolve the image of Padmasambhava and meditate on the emptiness nature, that is a form of vipashyana practice. Since guru yoga includes the practice of pure perception and the recognition of primordial wisdom, it is more extensive than shamatha or vipashyana. The discovery of pure perception, free from clinging and duality, comes from seeing Guru Padmasambhava's wisdom light reflecting in all directions. Guru yoga practice makes it possible to discover and experience everything as a radiant display of primordial wisdom.

The vajra, or dorje — symbol of the "diamond vehicle"

Vajrayana Meditation

The techniques of vajrayana meditation enable us to let go of our limited ideas about reality and to experience what is beyond the five senses. Usually, we decide whether something is true on the evidence of the five senses. If we perceive something through our eyes, ears, nose, tongue, or touch, we say that it exists; if we do not perceive it through our senses, we say it is not there. Among the objects of the five senses — forms, sounds, smells, tastes, and tangible objects, we give the most credence to what we perceive with our eyes and ears. But to what degree are the five senses reliable? Do they fully communicate the qualities of reality?

According to the vajrayana tradition, things can be known without being seen or heard. For example, by doing vipashyana practice one gains insight that enables you to see things never previously imagined. Our mental ability goes far beyond our current sense perceptions and thoughts. For instance, knowledge need not be limited to the present moment; it is quite possible to know events in the past and future as well.

In addition to extraordinary perceptions, there are many actions we could perform that go beyond ordinary ideas of reality. When great masters like Buddha Shakyamuni and Guru Padmasambhava realized the emptiness of all phenomena, they were able to do things like sit and walk in the sky and leave their handprints and footprints in solid rock. Anyone who has the same realization of the true nature can do these things.

To reach enlightenment it is necessary to go beyond our limited ideas and discover the wisdom nature. Among the vehicles taught by the Buddha, both the mahayana and the vajrayana lead to enlightenment; the main difference is that the mahayana is a more gradual path, whereas the vajrayana directly reveals the nature of the mind. Vajrayana meditation practice does this in two main ways: through creation stage practice and completion stage practice.

The creation stage uses visualizations to reveal that the universe, both internal and external, is pure light. In order to display the self-existing primordial wisdom, we have to transform old habits of perceiving whatever we see, hear, and touch as being solid and truly existent. In creation stage practice, we visualize a pure land containing pure deities and enlightened beings such as Vajrasattva or Guru Padmasambhava. When we meditate on the body of the deity, we perceive our own body transformed into a pure, absolute body, and we see that all sentient beings, ourselves and others, are pure and primordially enlightened. The visualization practices display the pure nature of reality. It is because of our mind's habitual ways of discriminating between things that we create a static world that is actually unreal. Visualization practice breaks our habitual, ignorant thinking so that we can experience the purity and equality of all phenomena and perceive their wisdom nature.

After making progress in the visualization practice, one does the completion stage meditation. The subtle completion stage practice applies to one's physical body. From the vajrayana point of view, the body is no longer seen as unpleasant or impure, rather it is considered to be totally enlightened. The structure of the body corresponds to the structure of the external world, and the body is recognized as the indestructible, vajra body, and as a vajra city filled with enlightened beings.

Practicing the subtle aspects of the completion stage is connected with the three main systems of the body: the channels, the wind, and the essence element. These three are closely interconnected; when one of them is clear it affects the others. The practices which focus on the channels release the knots of the channels so that the breath has a clear passage. In terms of the breath, the highest type of wind, called the subtle wisdom wind, can be made to pervade all the channels, and when that happens the essence element is also refined. The essence element is the most subtle or primordial element of the body, and when it is revealed through meditation practice the enlightened primordial awareness is also revealed.

The activities of enlightenment go far beyond ordinary concepts. According to both mahayana and vajrayana, the purpose of accomplishing enlightenment is to benefit all sentient beings. An enlightened being does not selfishly retire from the world, but becomes busier than before, without feeling even slightly burdened by the activities. Since enlightenment is all-pervasive, enlightened actions are as effortless and spontaneous as the light shining from the sun. Buddha activity transcends all ordinary ideas of effort and accomplishment.

There is more to reality than what can be perceived by our senses. The main reason for mentioning these advanced practices is to emphasize the precious opportunity that you have right now; if you practice meditation and develop your inner wisdom, you will be able to attain enlightenment and effortlessly help everyone in the entire world.

Lady Yeshe Tsogyal

The Tantric Tradition and Terma

Tantra is a Sanskrit word that means "continuity." Tantra refers primarily to the unchanging nature of the mind, which continues without interruption from beginningless time until final enlightenment. The scriptures that teach the unchanging, vajra nature of the mind are called the tantras, and the means used to directly reveal the mind's nature are known as the tantrayana or the vajrayana. Buddha Shakyamuni revealed many different types and levels of teaching to suit the various capacities of students. The highest section of his teaching is the vajrayana, which encompasses many practices such as the preliminary practices, the creation stage and completion stage practices, and mahamudra and dzogchen. All vajrayana practices are important in their own way. The vajrayana can be divided into six levels, with dzogchen as the sixth (and highest) level.

Sometimes students ask if there is a difference in the role of men and women in vajrayana Buddhism. In the vajrayana there is nothing that discriminates against women. All people have the same authority to become teachers and the same opportunity for realization. In the inner tantras there are fourteen samayas, and the fourteenth samaya says that you should not blame, criticize, or argue with women. It does not say that you should not criticize or argue with men, so in one sense, the vajrayana seems to appreciate women more than men. Here and in the East, most Buddhist teachers are men, but in Tibet there have been many highly respected women masters.

Tibet has become famous as a Buddhist country. In Tibet there are four major schools: the Nyingma school, the Kagyu school, the Sakya school, and the Gelug school. *Nyingma* means "the ancient ones," and it is the oldest of the four schools. The Buddhist teachings first came to

Tibet in the fifth century, which is known as the dawn of Buddhism in Tibet, and began to flourish during the time of Guru Padmasambhava, in the eighth century. The Kagyu and Sakya schools started in the eleventh century, and the Gelug school started in the fourteenth century. All of these schools developed from the same root and teach vajrayana Buddhism. The various schools do not contradict one another, but each has its own lineage of great meditators and scholars.

Many of the vajrayana teachings of Guru Padmasambhava were hidden in various parts of Tibet for the sake of future generations. These hidden treasures are called *terma* in Tibetan, and the people who reveal them are called *tertons*. The terma treasures include texts and ritual objects that were hidden by Guru Padmasambhava and Lady Yeshe Tsogyal in Tibet in the eighth century. Yeshe Tsogyal, one of Padmasambhava's nine heart students, attained enlightenment in one lifetime. Yeshe Tsogyal left signs of her accomplishment, such as writing verses in solid rock with her finger.

The terma teachings were written down mainly by Yeshe Tsogyal, as well as a few others teachers, as instructed by Guru Padmasambhava, for the sake of future generations who would be living in different situations. They were hidden throughout Tibet, many of them in inaccessible locations, such as inside rock mountains and under the water of lakes and rivers. They were placed there by masters like Yeshe Tsogyal, who did so by the power of her realization. In most cases, she did not actually travel to those places, but she hid them through the power of her mind.

The terma can be retrieved only through the meditative power of the tertons. There are 108 great tertons and one thousand lesser tertons in the Nyingma lineage. The tertons are very special and powerful people, who often have special dreams, even as children, in which they receive blessings and teachings directly from Guru Padmasambhava and Yeshe Tsogyal. When tertons meditate, they become very powerful. For instance, through their meditation on the inner winds they have what is called "swift feet," the ability to move very fast over long distances. The reason that the tertons have such power is because they have revealed their own inner wisdom.

The tertons are able to find the treasures and bring them out of their hidden locations without any difficulty. For example, when a treasure revealer arrives at a terma spot, the rock opens by itself and the terton removes a container made of precious stones, metal, or wood that holds the scrolls of teachings. Besides dharma texts, the tertons also extract ritual objects such as vajras, bells, phurbas, statues, and cloth. As soon as the terma is removed, the rock immediately closes and it appears as if it had never been opened. One cannot tell where the terma spots are unless the tertons mark them in a special way.

The terma texts are very unusual; they are small pieces of yellow paper rolled into tight scrolls. If you put these rolls of paper into a fire, they will not burn. These teachings are written in a special language called the symbolic language of the dakinis. These scrolls have just a few small signs, which are not Tibetan letters, but when the tertons look at the letters, they can transcribe long books from them. There are many of these hidden treasures in Tibet, and they are considered very special objects. For example, if you carry one of them with you, it will protect you. During the Chinese invasion of Tibet, the terma were known to protect people from bullets. Even in present day Tibet, great tertons continue to reveal the terma treasures.

Guru Padmasambhava

Guru Padmasambhava

It is very important for people who wish to follow the vajrayana teachings to have a connection with Guru Padmasambhava, the first main teacher of the tantric tradition in Tibet. Buddha Shakyamuni promised to be reborn in the form of Guru Padmasambhava in order to spread the vajrayana teachings in this world. The Buddha predicted Padmasambhava's activities nineteen times in the sutras and tantras. Just as predicted, Guru Padmasambhava was miraculously born in the middle of a lotus in northwest India, in the country of Uddiyana, eight years after Buddha Shakyamuni passed away, about 500 BCE.

Guru Padmasambhava appeared in the lotus as an eight-year-old boy. King Indrabhuti came to see him and asked him five questions: "Where did you come from? Who is your father? Who is your mother? What do you eat? What do you do?" Guru Padmasambhava answered, "I came from the unborn state, the dharmadhatu. My father's name is Samantabhadra and my mother's name is Samantabhadri. For food, I eat dualistic thoughts, and for work, I benefit all sentient beings." When the king heard these answers he was very pleased and asked Guru Rinpoche to come live in his palace as his son. Guru Padmasambhava went to the palace and stayed there for many years.

When he left the palace, he fulfilled a prophecy of Buddha Vajrasattva by traveling to many places in India, where he lived in cemeteries and did various forms of meditation. He was already enlightened, but he performed these practices to demonstrate that meditation leads to enlightenment.

Guru Padmasambhava is renowned for having eight great manifestations, such as Dorje Trollo and Senge Dradok. Some of the Indian kings and ministers were jealous of his abilities and tried to kill him. When they tried to drown him in a river, he leaped out and danced in the sky. On one occasion a king in northern India had Padmasambhava thrown into a huge fire. After three days the fire turned into a lake and Guru Padmasambhava was found sitting in a lotus in the middle of the lake. This spot has become a famous pilgrimage place in northern India; it is called Tso Padma, or the Lotus Lake. Padmasambhava's miracles influenced many beings to open their hearts to the dharma.

Another Indian king who had contact with Padmasambhava was King Ashoka, who had a large empire in Asia at one time. Earlier in his life he was very cruel and killed thousands of sentient beings. After meeting a manifestation of Guru Padmasambhava, he had a complete change of heart and promised he would never touch his sword again. He began to work for the dharma, sponsoring teachers and establishing the buddhadharma throughout southern Asia. It is said that Ashoka built a million Buddhist stupas in different parts of his kingdom.

In the middle of the eighth century, Guru Padmasambhava came to Tibet at the invitation of King Trisong Deutsen, the most powerful leader in Asia at that time. Trisong Deutsen was dedicated to establishing the dharma in Tibet and called upon Padmasambhava for help. Guru Padmasambhava subdued all the negative forces and blessed the entire land of Tibet. He consecrated the land and supervised the building of Samye Monastery, the first Tibetan monastery. By giving the vajrayana teachings in accordance with the individual needs and abilities of his students, many Tibetans attained enlightenment through his teachings and transmissions. Among his most famous students were the twenty-five close disciples, nine of whom were called his heart students, and the eighty great siddhas.

There are different accounts of how long Guru Padmasambhava stayed in Tibet. Most histories say that he stayed 111 years. This counts each waxing and waning of the moon as a separate month, which means that he stayed in Tibet for fifty-five years and six months. Other histories say that he stayed for only six months or eighteen months or a few years. Some people say that he spent only a few months in Lhasa and the rest of the time in the mountains and caves in the countryside. It could appear in different ways because Padmasambhava's crazy wisdom activities do not necessarily conform to our usual concepts. These events took place over a thousand years ago, and even in recent history scholars disagree and write different accounts about what has happened.

There is a particular reason for saying that Guru Rinpoche stayed fifty-five and a half years in Tibet. After finishing Samye Monastery, Padmasambhava and Khenpo Shantarakshita said that they were ready to go back to India. King Trisong Deutsen asked them to stay until his death for the sake of the Tibetan people. Both teachers agreed, and Padmasambhava stayed for an additional five years after Trisong Deutsen's death to help the king's sons continue the Buddhist tradition.

On the day of his departure from Tibet, Padmasambhava's students and the current king and courtiers went with him to a mountain pass named Gungthang Lathog on the border of Tibet and Nepal. He stopped at the mountain pass and said that no one should follow him further. All the people became very emotional, and as he began giving his final teaching he levitated and continued teaching from the sky. A horse appeared in the air and he mounted the horse and rode off in the western direction. Guru Padmasambhava did not die in the way that we normally think of death, rather he was able to transmute all the gross elements of his body into wisdom light. This is called attaining the rainbow body, and it is a state of wisdom beyond birth and death.

When he left, Padmasambhava said he was going to a country filled with cannibals whom he would teach to be bodhisattvas. Yeshe Tsogyal later reported that he reached his destination. Many great meditators have reported visiting him there in the land called the Glorious Copper-Colored Mountain. We cannot tell the exact geographic location of this land; it is similar to the kingdom of Shambhala in that way. According to

Buddhist cosmology there are four major continents and eight subcontinents. The Copper-Colored Mountain is one of the subcontinents. The histories say that he returned to Tibet many times to see Yeshe Tsogyal and to give teachings to later great masters. All the great tertons have had the experience of meeting Guru Padmasambhava in dreams, in visions, or in person. In their biographies they report going at least once to the Copper-Colored Mountain, where they obtained instructions and then returned and revealed the teachings they received to others.

Guru Padmasambhava hid many terma, or treasure teachings, in different parts of Tibet for the sake of future generations. Among the terma he included many predictions about the future of our world. Some of the predictions are about Tibet only and some are about other areas of the world. He predicted what would happen from generation to generation and how many of the problems could be solved. For many centuries these teachings have been very beneficial because his predictions are so accurate. Some people in the West have heard one of his clearest predictions: "When the iron bird flies and horses run on wheels, the dharma will go to the land of the red man."

Not all of the texts composed by Guru Padmasambhava are terma. Some of them are *kama*, the oral transmission written down in regular books. A few of his kama texts are *The Garland of Pith Instructions on the View*, a commentary on the *Guhyagarbha Tantra* called *The Blazing Light of the Sun and Moon*, and another tantric commentary, *The Ornament of the Cemetery Cuckoo*. Another text, which discusses working with wild feminine spirits, is *How to Balance the Activities of the Mamos*.

Guru Padmasambhava holds a special place among the Tibetan Buddhist schools, most of which trace transmissions and blessings directly from him. He is an embodiment of all enlightened beings. Of course, all the buddhas work for the benefit of sentient beings, but because Guru Padmasambhava made the vajrayana teachings available to us, he is considered to be the special buddha of our era.

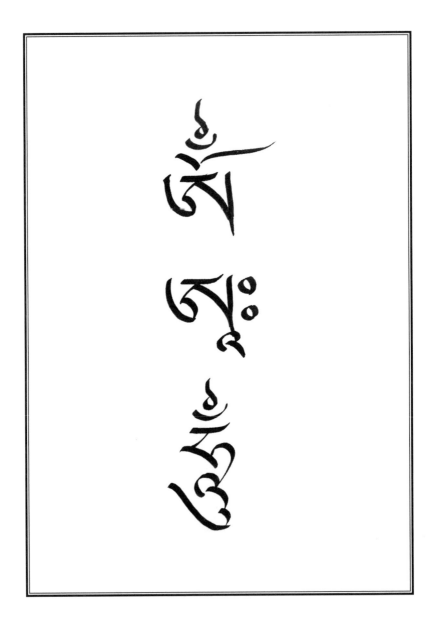

*OM AH HUNG, seed syllables of enlightened body, speech, and mind
(calligraphy by Khenpo Tsewang Dongyal Rinpoche)*

Guru Yoga Practice

All of the Buddha's teachings are like stairsteps leading to dzogchen, the great perfection, which is the summit of the vajrayana. The key that opens the door to dzogchen is the practice of guru yoga. If you want to practice dzogchen, you should first practice on Guru Padmasambhava, and then you will easily understand the dzogchen teachings. When you supplicate Guru Padmasambhava with a clear and peaceful mind, filled with devotion and bodhichitta, then his blessings and those of all the buddhas and bodhisattvas will help you to realize the true nature of your mind. For people who want to do vajrayana meditation it is very important to practice guru yoga.

Guru Padmasambhava represents the three jewels and the three roots — all of the objects of refuge. When you meditate on him you are not ignoring the other realized beings, because he embodies all of the buddhas of the ten directions and the three times. In particular, he represents your personal teachers and all of the masters of the Nyingma and Kagyu lineages. It is not necessary to visualize all the different buddhas; doing guru yoga and practicing on one buddha is enough to bring full enlightenment. Sometimes students wonder whether the meditation deities are simply created by the mind or whether they have a reality beyond the individual mind. All of them are existing buddhas as well as displays of our own wisdom. You can focus on the meditation deities to whom you feel the strongest connection and you do not have to practice on all of them.

A simple yet complete way to meditate on Guru Padmasambhava is to recite the Seven-line Prayer and the Vajra Guru Mantra. The preparation for guru yoga practice is the same as for sitting practice. Start with three prostrations to the shrine, then sit down with good posture on a cushion and do the breath purification exercise three times. Although it is beneficial to have a shrine, it is not mandatory — wherever you meditate with good motivation is your shrine.

Then, visualize in the space in front of you, a little above the level of your eyebrows, a lotus with five-colored petals. Above the lotus is a sun and moon seat on which Guru Padmasambhava sits in the royal posture. He has one face, two arms and two legs. His white, youthful body is a wisdom body made of light; it is not made of substantial flesh and bone. He is sitting in a five-colored, circular rainbow that is radiating wisdom light in all directions. See Guru Padmasambhava smiling down at you with compassion and loving-kindness. At this point take refuge and then arouse bodhichitta, the intention to attain enlightenment for the benefit of all beings. In this practice, while you are visualizing Padmasambhava with devotion, you are also cultivating compassion and loving-kindness for all beings.

After the refuge and bodhichitta, recite the Seven-line Prayer at least three or seven times. The Seven-line Prayer is very powerful. It was not composed by human beings; it came from the voice of the true nature, the dharmadhatu state. At the moment when Guru Padmasambhava was born in the lotus, hundreds of wisdom dakinis surrounded him and chanted these lines.

The Vajra Guru Mantra, OM AH HUM VAJRA GURU PADMA SIDDHI HUM, has twelve Sanskrit syllables which represent internal and external aspects of our existence. For example, in the Tibetan calendar, time is grouped in units of twelve — there are twelve signs of the zodiac, and cycles of twelve years, twelve months, and twelve hours. In Buddhism there are twelve links of interdependent origination and twelve acts of a supreme buddha. These groups of twelve are all connected, purified, and balanced by this mantra.

Even one recitation of the Vajra Guru Mantra has great benefit; it is not the same as repeating ordinary words. When you do this practice, recite the twelve-syllable mantra for as long as you have time. You should repeat it at least twenty-one times, or for one mala of 108 repetitions, or for ten malas, or one hundred malas — whatever you can do. If you are in a hurry to see Guru Padmasambhava, then you should do more. You could begin by reciting the mantra at least 108 times per session, with the goal of reciting the mantra a total of one hundred thousand times.

The sound of the mantra is also meditation, and you can use it as a technique to aid your practice. By concentrating on reciting the mantra musically, you can purify the channels and bodily systems. As well as keeping the inner levels in proper balance, mantra recitation purifies external situations. You can use this technique to turn the whole world into a mandala of music.

When you finish the mantra recitation you receive the blessings of Guru Padmasambhava. To do this, visualize seed syllables made of light in Guru Padmasambhava's three centers: at his forehead is a white OM, at his throat is a red AH, and at his heart center is a blue HUM. Visualize a strong white light, like a shooting star, coming from the syllable OM in Guru Padmasambhava's forehead and entering your forehead. It brings the blessings of the vajra body and removes your body obscurations. Red light, as powerful as lightning, comes from the syllable AH in his throat and enters your throat, conveying the blessings of vajra speech, which remove the obscurations of your speech. A piercing blue light from the syllable HUM at his heart enters your heart and you receive the blessings of vajra mind, so that your mental obscurations are removed. With this you should feel that all the subtle obscurations of your body, speech, and mind are gone and that you fully receive the blessings of Guru Padmasambhava.

At the end of the practice, visualize that Guru Padmasambhava dissolves into white light. This light moves until it is directly above you, then it enters your body through the top of your head and descends to your heart, filling your body with wisdom light that merges with your awareness. As much as you can, feel at that moment that your body is no longer solid, but has become a body of rainbow light. Remain inseparable from the wisdom of Guru Padmasambhava without being distracted by thoughts for as long as you have time. Then, conclude by dedicating the merit of your practice for the benefit of all sentient beings.

There are many ways to meditate, but no matter which technique you use, you need to apply concentration. This involves keeping the mind on the object of focus. For example, when you recite mantras, you can concentrate on visualizing each syllable of the mantra circling around like it is written on a wheel. Concentrating on each syllable while reciting the mantra helps to transform ordinary speech into vajra speech, and at the same time you are developing the ability to concentrate in meditation. Also, during meditation you need to apply mindfulness, to watch what your mind is doing, as a support for your concentration. This is the basic instruction for beginning your daily practice.

When you do vajrayana practice it is very important to establish a personal connection with a lama and with Guru Padmasambhava. By connecting with Guru Padmasambhava you receive his assistance in understanding the true nature of the mind. Doing guru yoga practice also brings a very close connection to your personal teacher, who exemplifies the realization gained by the practice. When you connect with a personal teacher, you have an auspicious situation similar to that of Guru Padmasambhava's twenty-five disciples, all of whom became enlightened by following the instructions of their teacher.

Ratna Lingpa

Advice on Visualization

Sometimes when students are learning to visualize they find it difficult to maintain the visualization. Since the meditation deities are displays of primordial wisdom, their images are not solid objects. For instance, Guru Padmasambhava manifests in many different ways; his form and color are not definite. Sometimes Guru Padmasambhava might transform into a small bird who is singing outside your window. Sometimes he appears and sometimes he disappears. When his body of primordial wisdom disappears, you should not worry that you have lost touch with him; continue your meditation so that Guru Padmasambhava will come back again and again and become more clear.

The famous terton Migyur Dorje gave some advice about this. Migyur Dorje became a great master at an early age; he was only eleven years old when he began to discover terma. At the age of fifteen he told his students that Padmasambhava did not always look the way the paintings and statues depicted him. Sometimes he would look that way, but at other times he would appear in different forms and perform different activities, so the students should not expect him to always appear in the same way.

There is a famous story about the way Guru Padmasambhava looked when he first appeared to Ratna Lingpa. Ratna Lingpa was a terton who lived in the fifteenth century. When he was born there were many auspicious signs that indicated he was a very special child. His family was wealthy and when he grew up he married and lived as a householder; he never studied in a scholarly fashion. He was twenty-four years old when he first saw Guru Padmasambhava.

In many villages in Tibet, when people are young they get together to have parties that last all day and into the evening. During the daytime they do sports like archery, and at night they dance and sing and drink chang, the Tibetan beer. The day before Ratna Lingpa saw Guru Padmasambhava, he had spent the day and night at a party with the young people of his village. The next morning he went out to take care of his animals. Since he was quite rich, he had yaks and sheep as well as farm land.

He put the animals on the grassland to graze, and then he sat down to copy a biography of Guru Padmasambhava. This particular biography was discovered by another famous terton named Nyang-ral Nyima Ozer. It contains a very great prayer as well as a biography of Padmasambhava. Ratna Lingpa was very interested in having a copy of this chant so he could use it in his practice. As he sat there writing out the text, because of the archery and drinking and dancing the previous day he felt very tired and fell asleep. When he woke up he felt different; he felt joyful and fresh, and he looked up and saw a little old man standing in front of him. The man had a long beard and long hair and was wearing a robe made of yellow cotton cloth. In Tibet they usually do not wear cotton. They wear woolen material, even in the summer, because it is so cool. But this old man was wearing cotton cloth and just standing there. Ratna Lingpa did not know how the man could have gotten there.

Immediately, the man picked up the text that Ratna Lingpa was copying and said, "This is the biography of Guru Padmasambhava discovered by the great terton Nyang. Do you have devotion to Guru Padmasambhava?" Ratna Lingpa answered, "Yes, since I was born I have had a special and unchanging devotion for him. That is why I am copying this. I am going to chant it as part of my practice." And the man said, "Oh, that is quite good; you are quite a good person." Then, the old man jumped up, looked around and then asked, "Is there a mountain near here called The Hovering of the Garuda?" Ratna Lingpa answered that he did not know of any mountain named The Hovering of the Garuda, but he pointed to a far mountain that was called Garuda

112

Mountain. The old man said, "Yes, that's it," and then he pulled out a roll of paper from his chuba, which is a kind of Tibetan dress, similar to a kimono, in which you can hold many things. He pulled a roll of paper from his chuba and told Ratna Lingpa to open it and read what it said. When Ratna Lingpa read it he found that it described him by name, telling the name of his parents, the year and place in which he was born, and that when he was grown he would discover the terma teachings. It predicted the entire course of his life.

When Ratna Lingpa read this he felt very joyful, but at the same time he thought that it could not really be about him — it must be about someone else. But the letter even described the marks on his body. The letter also contained advice about what he should do in order to discover the terma. Because he was so happy, he said, "This is wonderful. May I copy this?" And the man said, "You do not have to copy it; I am giving it to you. You should keep it."

By then it was midday, and Ratna Lingpa asked the yogi to come to his house to have lunch and rest. Since the yogi looked a little cold, Ratna Lingpa wanted to offer him some warmer clothes. They went to Ratna Lingpa's home, but the yogi said he preferred to stay outside. Ratna Lingpa brought him butter tea, tsampa, chang, meat and cheese and offered it to him. Before eating, the yogi said many prayers and made offerings. After lunch he gave Ratna Lingpa a lot of advice about following the instructions on the rolled paper.

Since it was getting late and there were not any villages nearby, Ratna Lingpa invited the yogi to stay overnight so that he could reach another village during daylight. But the yogi would not stay. Ratna Lingpa said, "The night will be very cold and you do not have much clothing. I would like you to take my new wool chuba and some food." But the yogi refused, saying, "No, I will not need them where I am going. It is time for me to leave now." They began walking and after a few steps the yogi stopped and said, "You must remember all the advice I have given you.

113

You must have constant, pure devotion and continue to pray to Guru Padmasambhava. Always follow the instructions I gave you today."

Then, he gave a few hints to show that he was Guru Padmasambhava. He did not say, "I am Padmasambhava," but he gave some hints. Then, he pulled a small horn from his chuba and blew it in different directions. The moment he did that, he disappeared. When Ratna Lingpa saw that the yogi had disappeared, he thought that maybe the yogi was a magician and that the rolled paper he had placed on his shrine would be gone. He ran inside to check, and saw that the paper was still there.

After his meeting with the yogi, Ratna Lingpa's whole demeanor and outlook changed. He was always very happy and his mind remained in the natural state. Even the vibration of his house changed. That evening when his wife came home, she immediately asked why he looked so radiant. She noticed the house smelled different and wanted to know what had happened.

Ratna Lingpa felt he should not tell her everything that had happened. The yogi had told him that he should keep their meeting secret for three years. His wife kept insisting, and Ratna Lingpa was so happy that he finally showed her the roll of paper and explained how it had been given to him. Both of them kept this a secret for three years as he had been instructed. After three years, Ratna Lingpa began to discover terma in many places in Tibet.

This illustrates how Guru Padmasambhava can appear in a different form, as a little old man wearing yellow cotton cloth.

Question and answer session with the Venerable Khenpos
at Padma Samye Ling

Questions and Answers

Q: What do you mean by sentient beings?

A: We are known as sentient beings because we have consciousness, or mind. Among the six main types of sentient beings, human beings are one of the highest. As human beings we are not superior because of our bodies; there are many animals who are stronger physically than we are. We are superior because our minds are highly developed.

Our mental ability is not something that we have to work to obtain; we have it naturally. Yet this ability can be developed further, perhaps further than we might expect. For example, we have technology today that was unimaginable only a few hundred years ago. Whereas modern people have more power over the external world, in ancient times people had more inner wisdom power. There are many stories from India and Tibet of people who could fly in the sky and walk through walls. Also, they had the power to change things like fire into water and water into fire.

It is because they developed their inner wisdom that people in the past could do those things. Today these powers are beyond our imagination; we think they must be fairy tales or myths. Likewise, if we could tell people from the past about the things we experience now, they might think our experiences are just myths. Yet both are possible, both outer and inner power can be developed by the mind. Material developments and inner wisdom are both reflections of our minds.

Q: When you talk about mind, you seem to include the emotions. How are they part of the mind?

A: The emotions are part of the relative level of the mind. We can divide the mind into many aspects; there are at least fifty-two mental factors. All of the emotions, such as anger, attachment, jealousy, pride, and doubt come from ignorance, which is also part of the mind. These strong obscurations keep the mind from remaining in the natural state. The emotions are part of the confused mind, which is unstable and always changing.

Q: If you maintain a clear and empty mind for a week or a month, is that enlightenment?

A: That is getting closer to enlightenment. Whatever amount you practice, even if it is only one or two hours, is working toward enlightenment. But you should not expect enlightenment after one week or month of practice.

Q: Do you think that meditation is the only way to reach enlightenment or do you think there are other ways?

A: Meditation is very important for attaining enlightenment, but I would not say it is the only way. You can meditate in different ways; you do not always have to sit still like a mountain to meditate. The Buddha taught many techniques for reaching enlightenment, but all of them are related to concentration and discipline.

Q: Do you have any advice on what to do when you realize you have not acted out of love and compassion, but have done something unkind?

A: Generally, recognizing that you did something wrong helps to purify your negative action and it decreases your tendency to act that way in the future. When you acknowledge your unkindness, your mind returns to the state of love, compassion, and wisdom, which can awaken you from further negativity. It is said that the only positive quality of negative action is that it can be purified. Recognizing that you behaved badly begins the process of purification; then you need to consciously decide that you are not going to act that way again.

Beyond having the intention to change your behavior, when you see that you have hurt others, you could do practices for them related to generosity, discipline, patience, and joyful effort. Concentration practices also help you become more pure and strong. The vajrayana meditation on Vajrasattva is particularly helpful in purifying negative actions.

Q: Rinpoche, would you tell us about your training?

A: I was born in eastern Tibet. When I was four years old I began to learn how to read. In Tibet it was not like here — there were no kindergartens or preschools. Instead, we would go to a master who had only a few students. I had a master and other teachers as well, and sometimes my parents would teach me. As children we did not have the number of toys that you have here. We had a few toys, but we really did not have time to play with them. My time was spent studying. In Tibet your thoughts were your toys.

Learning to read Tibetan was considered very important, so we learned to read very quickly. We learned reading in three stages: alphabet, pronunciation, and spelling. After that came formal reading and the study of grammar. I also had to write in Sanskrit, using the ancient Sanskrit letters, which are different from those used now. When I was about seven years old I started to learn and memorize certain rituals. In Tibet we memorized the words and the meaning of many texts, which we had to repeat to the master. We also studied history and the biographies of Buddha Shakyamuni and Guru Padmasambhava.

I did that until age twelve, when I went to a large monastic university, where we learned the five major sciences and the five minor sciences. First, we studied the early Theravadin teachings, which were brought to Tibet in about the eighth century, and then the mahayana teachings, and later, the vajrayana and dzogchen. I also learned astrology, medicine, art, and geometry. I studied there for about ten years, until I was twenty-one.

At that time we were having problems in Tibet because of the

Communist Chinese invasion. There was guerrilla fighting in Eastern Tibet and it became so dangerous that we could not stay there. I left in 1960 and arrived in India in 1961. During that year I had some terrifying experiences, as horrifying as nightmares.

When I got to India I stayed in a refugee camp where I taught the children. In 1965 His Holiness the Dalai Lama called together the refugee Tibetan scholars and masters to ask us to keep alive the lineages and culture of Tibet. His Holiness Dudjom Rinpoche asked me to attend, so I went. The conference lasted for about a year, with seventy-five great masters and scholars in attendance. That was in 1965 and 1966.

In 1967 the Indian government helped to open the Institute of Tibetan Studies, which is dedicated to saving the culture and knowledge of the Tibetan people. The Indian government helped His Holiness Dudjom Rinpoche to start the Nyingmapa Studies Department at the Institute, and His Holiness asked me to teach there. From 1967 to 1983 I taught and helped organize that department at the Central Institute of Tibetan Higher Studies. When we started, I was head of the department and the only person teaching Nyingma Studies. I had many responsibilities, including teaching about twelve classes every day.

I first came to the United States in 1980, and came back again in 1983. Since then, I have been teaching in North America as well as in Europe and Australia. This is a brief account of my training.

Q: At what age do people begin meditating in Tibet?

A: In the Nyingma lineage in Tibet, the students started meditating at about age twelve, at the same time they began to learn the major sciences. It was only after I arrived in India in 1961 that my personal meditation practice developed. Sometimes in India I practiced for periods of two or three months. In 1966 or 1967 I had the opportunity to go to the mountains for my longest retreat of five months.

When I began studying with my master at the age of five, I saw him practicing in his meditation box. I was very small and did not know exactly what he was doing, but I was very interested. In the Tibetan tradition people often practice in wooden meditation boxes, which have backrests so that the practitioners can lean their heads back. I would stand on the porch and watch my teacher through the window. Since I did not have a beautiful box, I gathered some stones and tree limbs and made a crude box to sit in. I really did not know about meditation; I wanted to imitate my master.

Q: What is the role of faith in attaining liberation?

A: In Buddhism, faith is a combination of confidence and devotion. It is the feeling of confidence and joy in the truth of the teachings. There are different ways to develop faith. One way is through hearing the dharma or reading it. For example, when reading the life story of Buddha Shakyamuni or one of the great masters, you can suddenly feel great confidence and devotion deep within your heart. Sometimes faith in the dharma is developed through your own wisdom; nothing external is needed — you simply see that the teachings must be true. For example, when you see that the world is impermanent and that everything exists through causes and conditions, you develop a feeling of certainty or faith through your own wisdom.

As for liberation, it is called *tarpa* in Tibetan. Tarpa means that you have completely removed all your suffering and confusion. You do not have to go somewhere else to do that; liberation is right here when you have removed your ignorance and have power over your own mind.

Q: Was the historical buddha, Buddha Shakyamuni, the first person to become enlightened?

A: No, Buddha Shakyamuni was not the first enlightened being. The Buddha taught in the mahayana teachings that there are thousands of buddhas in all directions. Also, every sentient being has the seed or potential for enlightenment. Buddha Shakyamuni taught that the first buddha is really the primordial state of one's own mind. Since there is no buddha before one's own primordial nature, we sometimes call the true nature "the primordial buddha."

Q: Is mindfulness the primordial nature?

A: Mindfulness is not the primordial nature, but it is part of it. Mindfulness is a technique, which is said to be the best helper for reaching the primordial state. Once we reach the primordial nature, then mindfulness radiates from that. Just as the sun has many rays, mindfulness is one ray emanating from the primordial nature.

Q: What do you mean by the primordial nature of the mind?

A: In the higher levels of the Buddha's teaching it is said that all the phenomena we perceive are simply displays of the mind. The deepest nature of the mind, the enlightened mind, is known as primordial awareness. All mental activities arise from primordial awareness, and if we recognize that, then enlightenment manifests in every thought and perception. If we do not recognize it, then thoughts and perceptions continue to be obstructions that cause suffering.

In order to awaken inner wisdom, it is necessary to break down the dualistic concepts that posit an internal subject and external objects. Typically, we perceive ourselves as individual subjects who experience objects that are separate from the self; we feel distance and make distinctions between the two. The feeling of being a subject who relates to objects is simply a notion of the mind. The mind alone creates the concept of a separate self. Once that conception is formed we hold on to it, although from the primordial point of view the self does not really exist. To overcome duality it is necessary to cultivate the equanimity that encompasses both subject and object. Practicing love and compassion is extremely helpful in terms of understanding the inseparability of outer and inner reality.

To recognize everything as the perfect activity of the enlightened mind is to realize the primordial nature of pure awareness. Sometimes this is called *rigpa*. Rigpa is the innermost, true nature of the mind, our awareness which is fresh, uncompounded, and very open. Along with emptiness, rigpa contains clarity, loving-kindness, wisdom, and skillful means.

Meditation reveals this awareness that we all have. To recognize the movements of the mind as the display of wisdom and to let thoughts arise and go their own way is called the natural flow of awareness. Maintaining the natural flow of pure awareness is known as the king of meditation, the supreme understanding. This is the best way to practice as we meditate, chant, and recite mantras.

The meditation on Guru Padmasambhava, the embodiment of all enlightened beings, is a practical way to invoke primordial wisdom. The word *buddha* means the primordial awareness that consists of love, compassion, and wisdom. When we visualize Guru Padmasambhava and chant the Vajra Guru Mantra, our potential wisdom is reflected in his image. The point of all practice is to bring out the primordial nature of the mind. When we are completely in the state of primordial wisdom, then that is enlightenment.

Q: What is the relationship between dzogchen and bodhichitta?

A: The dzogchen teachings are the highest teachings of Buddha Shakyamuni. From the dzogchen point of view, everything is totally equal in one profound state, without duality and distinctions. Dzogchen is the ultimate view of the true nature of mind, which includes love and compassion. When we practice dzogchen we develop compassion and loving-kindness; dzogchen practice cannot be separated from bodhichitta practice. We cannot ignore relative bodhichitta and accept absolute bodhichitta; both are part of our true nature and both are part of dzogchen.

123

For this reason, before we meditate, we take refuge and develop the thought of bodhichitta. After we meditate we dedicate the merit to all sentient beings. Whenever we practice or do any kind of beneficial activity, we should not cling to it. At the absolute level, everything is totally pure and perfect in great emptiness. From that point of view, we are completely free from all dualistic concepts and clinging.

Until we come to realize the emptiness nature, we continue to follow our thoughts, judging things to be good or bad, better or worse, dirty or clean. Even while we are following our thoughts, the ultimate reality does not change. It is similar to the weather. When you see a cloudy, gray sky, you cannot see the sun, but that does not mean that the sun and the blue sky are not there. They are still there; the moving clouds do not affect them.

Your thoughts are like the clouds that hide the sun of wisdom. When you reveal your inner wisdom and understand your primordial nature, all of your relative experiences become dreamlike. The objects you experience do not actually exist as the solid entities they seem to be. These dreamlike illusions are obscurations that come from your mind, and you must work with your mind in order to remove them. The obscurations cannot be burned away with fire or washed away with water, but they can be cleared away by bodhichitta and meditation. Bodhichitta and meditation are the best cleansers. When you practice with bodhichitta you will be able to reveal profound treasures never previously available to you.

Every person has the enlightened nature, but to actualize that nature it is necessary to practice bodhichitta, the love and compassion for all beings. Bodhichitta is universally precious; everybody appreciates it and everybody has the potential to develop it. Enlightenment is completely dependent upon developing compassion for all beings. The wish to attain enlightenment for the benefit of others is the essence of both the mahayana and vajrayana paths. When we develop inner wisdom, we can take care of all sentient beings, and radiate compassion and kindness throughout the universe. We can discover the true nature of the mind and of the entire world. In order to be able to do this, meditation practice is very important.

Bodhichitta is the root or the seed from which enlightenment develops. Bodhichitta is not found externally, but it is within your own mind. Although all of us have experienced love and compassion, these qualities need to be developed further. One way to increase them is to do the dzogchen meditation of resting the mind in its own nature. This is because bodhichitta and emptiness have the same nature, the true nature of the mind. Practicing bodhichitta openly and freely will increase your understanding of emptiness because compassion and emptiness are inseparable aspects of the primordial state of being.

DEDICATION

འཛམ་གླིང་སྤྱི་དང་ཡུལ་ཁམས་འདི་དག་ཏུ།

'dzam gling spyi dang yul khams 'di dag tu
DZAM LING CHI DANG YÜL KHAM DI DAG TU
At this very moment, for the peoples and nations of the earth,

ནད་མུག་མཚོན་སོགས་སྡུག་བསྔལ་མིང་མི་གྲགས།

nad mug mtshon sogs sdug bsngal ming mi grags
NE MUG TSÖN SOG DUG NGAL MING MI DRAG
May not even the names "disease," "famine," "war," and
"suffering" be heard.

ཆོས་ལྡན་བསོད་ནམས་དཔལ་འབྱོར་གོང་དུ་འཕེལ།

chos ldan bsod nams dpal 'byor gong du 'phel
CHÖ DEN SÖ NAM PAL JOR GONG DU PEL
But rather may pure conduct, merit, wealth, and prosperity
increase,

རྟག་ཏུ་བཀྲ་ཤིས་བདེ་ལེགས་ཕུན་ཚོགས་ཤོག །

rtag tu bkra shis bde legs phun tshogs shog
TAG TU TA SHI DE LEG PÜN TSOG SHOG
And may supreme good forune and well-being always arise.

By His Holiness Dudjom Rinpoche

Index of Illustrations

All illustrations used with the kind permission of the artists.

Padmasambhava Buddhist Center

Khenchen Palden Sherab Rinpoche and Khenpo Tsewang Dongyal Rinpoche have established Padmasambhava Buddhist Center to preserve in its entirety the authentic message of Buddha Shakyamuni and Guru Padmasambhava, and in particular to teach the tradition of Nyingmapa and Vajrayana Buddhism. They are dedicated to world peace and the supreme good fortune and well being of all. For more information about the Venerable Khenpos' activities, Padmasambhava Buddhist Center, or Dharma Samudra Publishing, please contact us at:

Padma Samye Ling
618 Buddha Highway
Sidney Center, NY 13839
(607) 865-8068

www.padmasambhava.org